This Day and Always

INSPIRATIONAL MESSAGES FROM
"MUSIC AND THE SPOKEN WORD"

GIVEN BY
LLOYD D. NEWELL

DESERET BOOK COMPANY
SALT LAKE CITY, UTAH

Published by Deseret Book Company, P. O. Box 30178, Salt Lake City, Utah 84130.

Deseret Book is a registered trademark of Deseret Book Company.

Library of Congress Cataloging-in-Publication Data

Newell, Lloyd D., 1956–
    This day and always : inspirational messages from "Music and the spoken
word" / given by Lloyd Newell.
     p. cm.
    Includes bibliographical references and index.
    ISBN 1-57345-473-7 (HB)
    1. Christian life—Mormon authors. 2. Meditations. I. Music and
the spoken word (Radio program). II. Title.
BX8656.N482   1999
242—dc21   99-10522
                                           CIP

Printed in the United States of America   10246-4728A

10   9   8   7   6   5   4   3   2

Contents

Adversity

Attitude

Beauty

Change

Contents

Choice

Compassion

Courage

Death

Faith

Contents

Family

Forgiveness

Friendship

Gratitude

Hope

Contents

Judging

Life

Love

Memories

Music

Patriotism

Contents

Peace

Self-Worth

Service

Simplicity

Spirituality

Contents

· A D V E R S I T Y ·

Our Trials Can Be Steps to Heaven

LIFE'S PURIFYING PATHWAY OF TRIALS, temptations, and afflictions provides daily opportunities for personal growth. Woven into the tapestry of each life are times when our suffering seems senseless or unnoticed—days that our burdens feel heavier than we can bear with mournful moments spent in death's dark shadow. At times we may even question how a loving God could allow us to feel such heart-wrenching pains, to endure such devastating losses, or to face such overwhelming challenges. When we are confronted by these trials, it is our courage and faith that can transform our suffering into personal growth and soften even our deepest sorrows.

Although God sees our struggles and hears our prayers, He does not always remove our challenges. In His loving wisdom, He would not deprive us of the very learning opportunity that life is meant to provide. Like gold that is purified by the refiner's fire and diamonds that are formed in extremes of stress and pressure, God knows that we will never attain the full stature of our souls without being stretched and scarred, tested and tried, in the crucible of life. As Neal A. Maxwell wrote, "Our trials and our experiences in life must be real. . . . The agony, the growth, the testing, and the joy must be real—real enough that they call forth in us [traits] that can only be mobilized under such conditions."[1]

Trusting that God will not allow us to be tempted or tried beyond what we can endure,[2] we can begin to see our trials as indications of His great trust in our capacity and potential. And while we would never choose the trials life forces upon us, we can always learn from them. By bravely enduring our trials, we learn humility, compassion for others, and a great reliance on God. We also learn that our happiness and progress depend much less upon what challenges life may bring and infinitely more on how we face and overcome those challenges. Looking back, we may even recognize that our personal trials and tragedies enabled us to gain new strengths and to learn important lessons that a loving Father in Heaven could teach us in no other way. What the caterpillar once saw as the end of the world, a butterfly later remembers as the time beautiful new wings grew, opening a world previously unimaginable.

God lifts us by allowing obstacles to block our paths from time to time. Often, He uses the very problems that slow our progress forward as His loving invitation to continue our journey upward. Our Father in Heaven has given us the chisel of determination and the hammer of faith so that we can carve steps in all our trials and climb one step at a time until we return to Him.

1. Neal A. Maxwell, *That My Family Should Partake* (Salt Lake City: Deseret Book, 1974), 67.
2. *New Testament,* 1 Corinthians 10:13.

Finding Solace for the Soul

THERE IS OFTEN AN UNSETTLING suddenness when storms blow in—as black clouds consume a blue summer sky, hail beats upon the earth without warning, or a clear winter's night gives way to a blinding blizzard.

And so it is with so much of life. Without warning, a child is taken ill; unexpectedly, an accident upends our world; with no time to prepare, a loved one's life is taken.

As much as we may wish for an endless array of sunny days and gentle evening breezes—and despite our understandable efforts to stay far from harm's way—most of us are perceptive enough to recognize that, with or without warning, thunder will one day roll across our skies and lightning will strike.

Are we wise enough, though, to prepare for such a day?

As we anticipate adversity, do we recognize it as a natural outgrowth of our mortal realm, or will our attitudes lead us toward anger and resentment when trials come? Are we inclined to ask, "Why me?" or "How could this have happened?" or will we focus instead on what we can learn and how we can grow? Do we see ourselves as victims, as being acted upon, or do we recognize the great gift of agency that enables us to choose how we'll respond to tragedy?

Martin Luther King Jr. once observed, "The ultimate measure of a man is not where he stands in moments of comfort and convenience but where he stands at times of challenge."[1] Unpredictable though they may be, such times can either break down a soul or lift one to greater strength and insight.

But we must never leave where we stand to chance, for, as C. S. Lewis has written: "You never know how much you believe anything until its truth or falsehood becomes a matter of life and death to you. It is easy to say you believe a rope to be strong and sound as long as you are merely using it to [tie] a box. But suppose you had to hang by that rope over a precipice. Wouldn't you then first discover how much you really trusted it?"[2]

Finding strength and solace for our souls should be an ongoing effort as we look out over clear skies, not a desperate act we undertake only as we find ourselves being buffeted by the storms at sea. Scripture teaches us something of the process—that "hope cometh of faith, [and] maketh an anchor to the souls of men."[3] And thus fortified, we are all the more prepared to partake of the divine promise, "Come unto me, all ye that labour and are heavy laden, . . . and ye shall find rest for your souls."[4]

1. Martin Luther King Jr., *Strength to Love* (New York City: Harper and Row, 1963), 20.

2. C. S. Lewis, *A Grief Observed* (New York City: Seabury Press, 1961), 25.

3. *Book of Mormon,* Ether 12:4.

4. *New Testament,* Matthew 11:28–29.

Daybreak Comes

LIFE IS RICH WITH SYMBOLISM. If we look carefully, evidence of God's love is all around us. The very passing of time—as night unfolds into dawn—reminds us that, even in our darkest hour, we can know that despair will not last forever and morning will surely come.

None of us eludes disappointment in this life. Sometimes our trials seem to roll over us as steadily as waves over sand. We suffer losses and setbacks, and we grieve with those we love.

Yet, just as God has balanced night with day, we can look for joy as vast as our sorrows. He has not left us in utter darkness. Just as sunlight bathes the earth each morning, so will our Father in Heaven part the shadows and bring radiant light and comfort to gladden our hearts again. Thunder gives way to cleansing rain; clouds give way to rainbows. Winter warms into spring, and barren branches fill with blossoms and the promise of fruit to come.

Nature resounds with evidence that God is tending His garden and watching lovingly over His children. He has given the Spirit of comfort to embrace us during times of need[1] and is only a prayer away.

Through trials, we develop faith in God—faith that He is our caring friend to help us through the adversities of life. And as we meet daily challenges, we acquire skills and knowledge. We gain perspective and learn which things matter most. We become more valuable to others as we now have the experience to help those with similar struggles. We discover that true joy comes through thinking of others before ourselves.

There will be nights of storm and darkness. There will be tears and aching hearts. But as we watch the morning sky and turn our hearts to God, daybreak comes.

1. *Book of Mormon*, Moroni 8:26.

Faith in the Future

IN THE CLASSIC MOVIE *The Wizard of Oz*, the young girl, Dorothy, faced a multitude of challenges that seemed at times to be overwhelming. During one of her moments of despair, she made a statement in song that expressed her wish for an easier time and a more perfect place.

> Somewhere over the rainbow,
> Skies are blue
> And the dreams that you dare to dream
> Really do come true.[1]

We all have dreams and desires. And we, too, sometimes wish for that elusive "somewhere over the rainbow." However, it seems to be the nature of life that the realization of dreams rarely comes easy. We all face challenges that seem to dash our dreams and leave us longing for a better day. It is during these times that we need to hold onto hope and trust that a better day does, indeed, lie ahead. It helps to believe, as British writer Tolkien did, that "still around the corner there may wait, a new road, or a secret gate."[2] This type of tenacious attitude can foster faith in the future and the ability to go on during the hardest of times—even with enthusiasm.

As downsizing takes place in many businesses today, those laid off face the devastating disappointment of losing the security of a job. This is one of those times when we can exercise faith in the future and walk that "new road." Many have found that a loss such as this has led them to more satisfying employment with far greater possibilities.

Even those of us who experience the loneliness that comes from the loss of a loved one through death or divorce can hold on and know that somehow we, too, will make it through. And though we may feel that no one or nothing can replace our loved one, still, by having faith in the future, we may find an unexpected "secret gate" that opens to a whole new world of peace and happiness.

Whatever it is we experience in this life, it is good to remember that life goes on and, with enough patience, prayer, and perseverance, things usually work to our advantage. Ralph Waldo Emerson said, "The whole of what we know is a system of compensations. Each suffering is rewarded, each sacrifice is made up, even debt is paid."[3] We need to have faith in the future and realize that sometimes it is the very hardships we experience that give us wings strong enough to fly over the rainbow and find our dream.

---

1. "Over the Rainbow," from *The Wizard of Oz,* words by E. Y. Harburg and music by Harold Arlen.
2. J. R. R. Tolkien, in *The Harper Book of Quotations* (New York City: HarperCollins Publishers, Inc., 1993), 326.
3. Ralph Waldo Emerson, *op. cit.,* 263.

To Journey with Joy

As LIFE UNFOLDS, WE EACH MAKE the discovery that it contains both ups and downs, good times and bad. Many of us mistakenly wish only for good fortune, hoping to sidestep adversity. On a list of what brings happiness, most people would include the elimination of all their problems.

But life's obstacles are no more predictable than the weather; rain and storms beset us all. And even if we could control all of our situations, this would not be the formula for genuine joy.

Happiness is not the result of circumstance. It is the result of loving others. Mother Teresa has long been a symbol of generous sacrifice. Her work with some of the poorest people of India has not only helped those individuals but has also inspired other people around the world.

Most who follow her example and devote a portion of time in Third-World countries are startled by the broad smiles that greet them from the midst of squalor and poverty. Such delight seems ironic to those of us from cultures which teach that it is material comforts that bring happiness.

And thus, we learn from those we came to teach: They may not have our technology or our training, but they have surpassed us in their understanding that joy comes from loving and caring for one another.

Throughout history our forefathers have expressed joy despite suffering. Immigrants and pioneers have led the way in every nation, sacrificing for those they loved. Their journals ring with courage, determination, faith—and happiness. As one group of pioneers sang, "No toil nor labor fear: but with joy wend your way."[1] Their goal was never personal comfort but to give their all that others might be blessed.

When love is what motivates us, trials do not stop us. We gather strength, we find solutions, and we march to victory. Said one, "Misfortune is great, but man is even greater than misfortune."[2]

The Apostle Paul wrote to the Corinthians of his many afflictions in standing up for his beliefs. On five separate occasions he was beaten with 39 stripes. But he rejoiced in his hardships, adversity strengthening him like fire tempering steel.[3]

When we sacrifice for love, when we demonstrate real courage, there is an invigorating joy that infuses our souls. This sense of happiness and peace stands in stark contrast to our circumstances, often puzzling those around us who have not climbed the same mountain. And yet, the sweet taste of victory over self cannot be denied. It doubles our strength and seems to lift us closer to God than we have ever before felt. It is exactly what Paul meant when he delighted in "distresses for Christ's sake: for when I am weak, then am I strong."[4]

Tests and trials will always be a part of life. But we can journey with joy, just as Paul did, if we remember the love of our Savior and show that same love for others.

1. William Clayton, "Come, Come, Ye Saints," *Hymns of The Church of Jesus Christ of Latter-day Saints* (Salt Lake City: The Church of Jesus Christ of Latter-day Saints, 1985), no. 30.

2. Rabindranath Tagore, in Dominique Lapierre, *The City of Joy* (New York City: Warner Books, 1985), 502.

3. *New Testament,* 2 Corinthians, chapters 11 and 12.

4. *New Testament,* 2 Corinthians 12:10.

· ATTITUDE ·

Happiness Is a Conscious Choice

THERE ARE TWO WAYS TO LOOK at life and the world. We can see the good or the bad, the beautiful or the ugly. Both are there, and what we focus on and choose to see is what brings us feelings of joy or feelings of despair. As a simple example, on a foggy day some people choose to complain about the inconvenience the fog causes, while others accept this occurrence of nature with anticipation for the beauty it brings. When it happens in a cold climate, the results *are* almost magical. As the fog lifts, it leaves moisture frozen to every branch on every bush and tree, and the effect is breathtakingly beautiful. Or, in a warmer climate by the sea, as the fog rolls in there is a mystic feeling of suspense and wonder as ships come from out of nowhere or as a setting sun, diffused by the mist, becomes a huge, enchanting red ball in the sky. What we see and enjoy is up to us.

So it is with some who see the crime and heartlessness that exist in the world. They conclude that, because of all the evil that is happening, there must not be a God. While, on the other hand, others see all the good that is being done and consider it just one more witness that there is a loving Creator reaching out to help in this mortal world.

In everything in life we can choose to find beauty and

9

goodness or complain about hardships and disappointments. Even in a marriage relationship we can choose to focus on the positive attributes of our mate, or we can be critical of imperfections that surely can be found in anyone. Beauty and joy can be brought into every relationship when we notice and nurture the good. We can grumble about our jobs, the boss, and the long hours—or we can look for the goodness, try to understand the struggle of an employer or fellow employees, and even rejoice in the very fact that we have a job with an income to provide for ourselves and loved ones.

We have the power to enjoy, even create, beauty in our everyday circumstances. Joy comes in so many different ways, and a generous measure of it lies within the grasp of every person. One man said: "Happiness is not always the result of fortune. . . . [It] comes of the grace to accept life gratefully and make the most of the best of it."[1] Happiness, then, becomes *our* conscious choice. Life becomes what we choose it to be.

1. Donald Culross Peattie, ed., *A New Treasury of Words to Live By* (New York City: Simon and Schuster, 1959), 27–28.

"Be of Good Cheer"

IN HIS FAMOUS BIOGRAPHY of Samuel Johnson, James Boswell quotes from a conversation between Johnson and a man named Oliver Edwards. Edwards makes the following observation: "I have tried too in my time to be a philosopher; but, I don't know how, cheerfulness was always breaking in."[1]

There are those individuals who seem to have a special gift for this kind of cheerfulness. They are the ones who, no matter how grim circumstances may be, retain a certain lightness of spirit. They are the ones who can see the comic potential of a given situation. They are the ones who laugh and invite the rest of us to laugh with them. They are the ones who, as the proverb notes, enjoy "a continual feast"[2] because of their merry hearts.

Spending time with people who possess the gift of good cheer can restore our souls. In their presence we begin to see the world the way they see it, so that the event we might ordinarily find tedious or irritating, stressful or sad, becomes somehow amusing—perhaps the basis for an anecdote to be shared with friends later on. E. B. White, author of the children's classic *Charlotte's Web*, notes that "there is a deep vein of melancholy running through everyone's life and that the humorist, perhaps more sensible of it than some others, compensates for it actively and positively."[3] When we are this type of individual, we laugh too. We enjoy ourselves and, ultimately, we feel better about our own lives.

People of good cheer come in all shapes and sizes. One may be the nine-year-old niece who's excited to teach you a new magic trick. Another may be the coworker who collects and shares silly jokes. Another may be the next-door neighbor who can survey all the messes of a hard day and find something to laugh about. Another still may be a wonderfully comic character in a book. Like good and faithful friends, these beloved personalities are there for us, ready and willing to make us smile.

No matter who they are, the people who lift our spirits deserve affection and our deepest thanks. We should cherish them always, for, in a very real sense, they help us to follow that divine admonition from long ago to "be of good cheer."[4]

---

1. James Boswell, *The Life of Samuel Johnson* (London: Penguin Books, 1986), 251.
2. *Old Testament,* Proverbs 15:15.
3. E. B. White, *Essays of E. B. White* (New York City: Harper & Row Publishers, 1979), 243.
4. *New Testament,* Matthew 14:27.

Bringing Light into Our Lives

W E LIVE IN AN IMPERFECT WORLD, and each of us, unwittingly or otherwise, makes our contribution to the conditions that we find intolerable. We may give voice to a grievance that would be better left unspoken; we may contend with another when we ought to walk away; we may succumb to bitterness rather than simply ignoring another's offense.

Then, ironically, we end up dismayed by the sorrows that surround us, by the pain that others are left to bear.

If we are ever to have peace in this life, we must begin by seeing ourselves as the starting point—not the neighbor with whom we quarrel, not some stranger who has crossed us, not the tyrant who rules a foreign land.

Instead, we would do well to remember the poet's prayer that God will "teach us tolerance and love."[1] For these two traits will take us a long way toward alleviating so many of the circumstances we so often lament.

But tolerance and love cannot be turned on and off according to our moods or whims; rather, they must be as much a part of our being as the heart that beats and sustains our every action.

Certainly, there are people who annoy us and situations that we deem intolerable. But we have the power within us to choose how we will respond to all that affects us. Experience would suggest that we are more inclined to give vent to those emotions that end in strife than to practice patience. Yet, tolerance and love suggest thoughtfulness instead of a rush to judgment, fellowship in place of a vaunted concern with self, agreement rather than discord, and the quiet calm that comes from a carefully chosen course of life.

In ancient times the Psalmist wrote: "Keep thy tongue from evil, and thy lips from speaking guile. . . . Do good; seek peace, and pursue it."[2] Such advice may seem too outdated to have any relevance in these tumultuous times, but its simplicity speaks a truth that still pertains today.

It is easy to view the conditions we face as beyond our control—or even beyond hope; but there is joy to be found in following basic truths, no matter how long they have been with us.

Then, rather than continually seeing dark clouds looming on the horizon, we can look to the east and see morning rays of sun that will warm our days and bring light into our lives.

1. Mabel Jones Gabbott, "In Humility, Our Savior," *Hymns of The Church of Jesus Christ of Latter-day Saints* (Salt Lake City: The Church of Jesus Christ of Latter-day Saints, 1985), no. 172.
2. *Old Testament,* Psalm 34:13–14.

"Strength in What Remains Behind"

OUR LIVES ARE FULL OF opportunities for growth, but oftimes we perceive these to be challenges and obstacles.

A small boy played along the seashore, gathering stones and piling them into heaps. His father walked down the shoreline, frowning intently, as though looking for something lost. When the child asked what he was doing, the father explained he was searching for an interesting stone. The boy looked surprised and admitted *he* had thought *all* the stones were interesting.

Sometimes we walk along life's path with our heads down, searching for something to lift our hearts and give us hope. Perhaps we are actually looking for something which gave us joy in the past. We may be listening for the voices of our children, who now live halfway across the country. Or we may feel the loss of strength and energy we once had, when we could work long hours without tiring or pursue a demanding hobby all weekend. We may spend so much time thinking and longing for what has passed that we overlook the many possibilities still before us.

In his twenties, Adrian was struck down with crippling arthritis. He was totally bedridden, with very limited use of his hands. He could turn his head only a few inches to the left or right and wore a headset to answer his telephone. When Jack, a friend from college days, came to visit, he expected to find Adrian bored and idle. Instead, he had to wait while Adrian finished several phone calls to students he was tutoring in math. In addition, Adrian was counseling troubled youth from his church. That evening a small group would be joining him to listen to and discuss a new jazz album. On the tray table, Jack saw drafts of letters Adrian was dictating to schoolmates now in the military service. Adrian admitted that some nights it was very late before he wound up his activities and went to sleep.

Adrian wasted little time longing for the pleasure and joys of the past. Instead, he gathered into his life a rich treasure of pursuits possible for him *today*. The poet William Wordsworth confirms that, while nothing can bring back those things that are past, "We will grieve not, rather find strength in what remains behind."[1] What better counsel than the words of the Psalmist, who reminds us, "This is the day which the Lord hath made, we will rejoice and be glad in it."[2]

1. William Wordsworth, "Ode: Intimations of Immortality," lines 179–80, in *The Norton Anthology of English Literature*, 6th ed. (New York City: W. W. Norton, 1993), 2:193.
2. *Old Testament*, Psalm 118:24.

Of Pennies, Our Thoughts, and Rainbows

W HEN I WAS SIX OR SEVEN YEARS OLD," writes Annie Dillard, "I used to take a precious penny of my own and hide it for someone else to find. . . . I was greatly excited . . . at the thought of the first lucky passerby who would receive in this way, regardless of merit, a free gift from the universe."[1]

Though exciting to a young girl, perhaps a token so small has become all but meaningless to most of us. Yet, in that "free gift" of the penny, there may be a lesson to be learned.

"The world," Dillard continues, "is fairly studded and strewn with pennies cast broadside from a generous hand. But . . . who gets excited by a mere penny?"[2]

Indeed, we often look beyond the small treasures of the world, beyond the hope and bright outlook so common among the young. Our minds, it seems, become clouded by pressures and pessimism, and we forget to look for the marvels and the good in the world around us because they are sometimes so difficult to find.

Matthew Arnold describes in verse the lack of hope we sometimes feel:

> The sea of faith
> Was once, too, at the full, and round
> earth's shore . . .
> But now I only hear
> Its melancholy, long, withdrawing
> roar.[3]

In truth, we choose what we will hear, what we will see, what we will perceive the world to be.

Without doubt, there is sometimes too much travail in our own lives, in the lives of family and friends, and in the world around us. We can always find enough excuses to turn from our faith and our hope. But we can also choose to see the bright pennies, those seemingly small treasures tucked between the cracks of a sidewalk or hidden beside a tree.

Though hope and a healthy optimism won't guarantee us a life devoid of difficulty, there is an abundance of good to be found in this world. And the attitudes we possess as we live each day will determine, in large measure, what we see and how we respond— whether we perceive only the problems or find the pennies, whether we see only gathering clouds of storm or wait patiently and look for the rainbow.

1. Annie Dillard, "Seeing," in Phillip Lopate, ed., *The Art of the Personal Essay* (New York City: Anchor Books, 1994), 693.
2. Ibid.
3. Matthew Arnold, "Dover Beach," in *The Norton Anthology of English Literature* (New York City: W. W. Norton and Company, 1962), 2:905.

· BEAUTY ·

Beauty

HOW DO WE MEASURE BEAUTY? What is its essence, its substance, its reality? From the beginning of time, people have looked at landscapes and paintings and words and declared them "beautiful"; even while philosophers have asserted that beauty is something purely subjective, a quality that exists only in the eye of the beholder. And yet, year after year, people pack their belongings into cars and travel to parks and vistas, canyons and waterfalls, museums and theaters to stare in wonder, to marvel together. At what? At this thing we call beauty.

What is this quality we call beauty? The Psalmist expressed a universal longing when he sang, "One thing have I desired . . . to behold the beauty of the Lord."[1] The truest earthly beauties speak of the marvelous creations of God—speak of God's goodness and love. As Gerard Manley Hopkins wrote: "Glory be to God for dappled things. . . . All things counter, original, spare, strange; he fathers-forth whose beauty is past change: Praise Him!"[2] God "fathers-forth" things of beauty. From the brown specks on the back of a brook trout to the clouds swirling about the peaks of Kilimanjaro, all the world speaks of the glory of His creation.

Man, too, is capable of beauty. Indeed, our poets and painters share in a small way the greatest of God's attributes—the ability to create, to mold and shape and breathe life into the clay of our existence.

We restore our spirits when we surround ourselves with beauty. Even the smallest and most unruly of children will cease their squabbling to stare in awe at a sunset or a mountain canyon. Even the weariest of travelers is refreshed by the sight of nature at her loveliest. Even those lost in the depths of despair can find comfort and solace in the creations of God or man.

We may not know just what beauty is. But our souls declare that beauty is always around us. And where we find beauty, we find the light of God.

1. *Old Testament,* Psalm 27:4.
2. Gerard Manley Hopkins, "Pied Beauty," in X. J. Kennedy, *Literature: An Introduction to Fiction, Poetry and Drama* (Boston: Little, Brown, 1966), 585.

Adding to the Divine Masterpiece

ASTRONAUTS, IN THE BLACKNESS of outer space, have observed in awe an ever-changing panorama of oceans, clouds, and continents and have marveled at the beauty and complexity of our planet. The deep blues and greens of the seas, the restless motion of the atmosphere, and the diversity of color and texture across the dry land comprise the divine masterpiece called Earth.

Whether from a celestial orbit—or at arm's length—our world abounds with evidence of the sensitivity of a loving Father in Heaven: the delicate shading on a tiny flower, the sweet smell of a newborn infant, the warm pinks and blues of a summer sunset.

One of God's most precious gifts to humankind is our opportunity to add our own beauty to that of the Creator. Within every human heart is planted the desire to make the world a better place. But, in such a big and complex world, how can only one person accomplish such a task? God has made that part simple, too. Within each of us is the ability to add more beauty and kindness to the earth in every moment we breathe: a smile during a traffic jam, a few more minutes with a child, a kind word, a soft answer, a wrong forgiven. With each new day, we can combine our own unique artistry to the beauty of all creation. If our hope is to make a better world, the realization is only a choice away. In the words of Og Mandino:

> I will love the sun for it warms my bones; yet I will love the rain for it cleanses my spirit. I will love the light for it shows me the way, yet I will love the dark for it shows me the stars. I will welcome happiness for it enlarges my heart; yet I will endure sadness for it opens my soul.[1]

A note of thanks, a warm embrace, a happy smile—these tiny, simple gestures add beauty on a grand scale and, in partnership with God, they make the world a better and a more beautiful place.

The ancient Psalmist and the astronauts of the modern age seem to agree, "The heavens declare the Glory of God; and the firmament sheweth his handywork."[2] And this day, even this hour, each individual soul can add his or her own beauty to the artistry of the Divine.

1. Og Mandino, *Three Volumes in One* (New York City: Bonanza Books, 1981), 52–54.
2. *Old Testament,* Psalm 19:1

In the Things of Nature, There Is the Marvelous

IN ALL THINGS OF NATURE," wrote Aristotle, "there is something of the marvelous."[1]

Whether we live in a rural setting or in a robust city, we needn't look far to find something that will lift our spirits and bring us closer to the soul of life.

Said Albert Schweitzer, "Never say there is nothing beautiful in the world. There is always something to make you wonder in the shape of a tree, the trembling of a leaf."[2]

Perhaps the splendid simplicity of a rose may clarify for us the innocent beauty of a child. Perhaps the weavings of a spider's web may point to the essential connections of all those who live upon this earth. Perhaps the brilliant sunrise may suggest something of the potential grandeur of the day that lies ahead.

In the words of the poet, "Go forth, under the open sky, and list to Nature's teachings."[3]

And, if we aren't seeing the beauty that surrounds us, we likely aren't looking around us. It may be that the noise of the city overwhelms the bird that is singing or that our concerns keep us from feeling the refreshment of a morning rain. Or could it be that our haste blocks from view the towering mountains or the oceans over which the sun is setting. Whatever the reason, we ought not be so wrapped up in our own little worlds that we fail to be inspired by the simple beauty of the world in which we dwell.

The naturalist John Burroughs has declared: "I am in love with this world. . . . It has been my home. It has been my point of outlook upon the universe. . . . I have tilled its soil, I have gathered its harvests. . . . [Yet] while I delved I did not lose sight of the sky overhead. While I gathered its bread and meat for my body, I did not neglect to gather its bread and meat for my soul."[4]

Similarly, while we, too, must till, we must not lose sight of the sky overhead. For if we will but look around us, we can, indeed, partake of the many marvels that will feed our hearts and souls.

---

1. Aristotle, in *Bartlett's Familiar Quotations*, 16th edition, ed. Justin Kaplan (Boston: Little Brown and Company, 1992), 77.

2. Albert Schweitzer, *The Words of Albert Schweitzer,* comp. Norman Cousins (New York City: Newmarket Press, 1984), 25.

3. William Cullen Bryant, "Thanatopsis," *The Poetical Works of William Cullen Bryant* (New York City: AMS Press, 1972), 21.

4. John Burroughs, "A Declaration of Devotion," in *Treasury of the Christian Faith* (New York City: Association Press, 1949), 321.

· CHANGE ·

Autumn Seasons and the Leaves of Life

WHEN THE LAST RAYS OF SUMMER herald the beginning of fall and the approach of winter, the leaves in many parts of the world change color. Beautiful and transitory, these colorful autumn leaves soon tumble to the ground, prompted by the coolness of shorter days or the capricious push of a passing breeze.

Like the trees, we will have autumn seasons in our lives. Life's seasons bring changes, and often the leaves that once seemed so much a part of us flutter off in the autumn wind or are stripped away by a sudden storm. Promotions fall through, jobs are lost, friends move away, loved ones die—at times it seems we lose the very things in which we've invested the most work and love. It takes very little living to learn few things in life are imperishable.

Sudden or anticipated, temporary or permanent, our losses in life are real and painful. At times, the winds of loneliness whistle around us, and the cold chill of despair fills our hearts. But the trees teach us. Stripped by conditions beyond their control of every sign of the warm summer days, the trees wait.

They have learned to weather the winter, to wait for the thaw, and to watch for the warmth and sunshine that accompany each returning summer, knowing that new growth and fresh spring blossoms are not possible until the seasonal circumstances remove the leaves and flowers of the past.

Yes, there will be autumn seasons in every life. Youth melts into old age, vigorous mental and physical capacities deteriorate, and financial stability can evaporate without warning; but the falling autumn leaves remind us that life is about growth, not accumulation. Eventually, we learn to look beyond what we have lost to recognize all that we have learned.

Like the trees, we cannot control everything that happens to us. Some aspects of our lives disappear, never to return. In other instances, our deprivations may be less permanent, and we are comforted by the knowledge that there are few matters of lasting consequence that God will not rectify in time.

When we learn to trust in spite of fear, to cope in spite of circumstance, and to bravely continue in spite of losses or disappointments, the leaves of our lives become tinted with lovely hues of courage, perseverance, and hope. They become a thing of enduring beauty regardless of where the breezes may carry them during one of life's autumn seasons.

That Which Is Changeless

UPON RECENTLY RETURNING to the town of his youth, one man reported that the changes he saw there left him breathless. The orchard through which he used to take shortcuts on his way to school was gone, replaced by a subdivision of homes. The field where he once played little league ball and dreamed boyish dreams of glory now boasted a shopping mall. And the drugstore where he used to buy comic books and sodas with friends on summer afternoons had given way to a sleek new office building. The trip home made the man acutely aware of the passage of time and the changes it inevitably brings.

Change. Everything changes. Towns change, styles change, seasons change, people change. We watch as our own parents move through the stages of their lives—from middle age, in which they are engaged in making their careers and raising their families, to retirement, and then, finally, to that time of life when one's closest companion becomes memory. We watch, too, as the children coming up behind us change from chubby toddlers to gawky youths to maturing young adults capable of negotiating the world on their own. And, of course, we see the changes in ourselves.

A Greek philosopher once said that "there is nothing permanent except change."[1] While change is certainly the constant feature of human experience, there are moments when we are overwhelmed by its relentless reality. On occasion, our mood may even mirror that of the melancholy speaker in the opening lines of Shakespeare's sonnet: "Like as the waves make toward the pebbled shore, So do our minutes hasten to their end."[2] At times like these, when we feel adrift in a sea of change, we yearn with the very marrow of our bones for something that remains the same.

There is one thing that never changes, and that is the love of God for each one of us. The love of God does not ebb and flow. It is not influenced by our appearance or by the amount of cash in our wallets, by our abilities or even by our actions. It is simply and profoundly *there*—there for us when we are filled with sorrow as well as joy, despair as well as hope, anger as well as peace. The love of God is there for us when we deserve love, and it is most especially there for us when we do not. It is there always, as fixed and firm as the mountains around us.

1. Heraclitus, in *The Harper Book of Quotations*, 3rd edition, ed. Robert I. Fitzhenry (New York City: HarperPerennial, 1993), 86.
2. *The Complete Works of Shakespeare* (Garden City, New York: Doubleday and Company, Inc., 1936), 1411.

"Till We Meet Again"

It HAS BEEN SAID THAT the only thing which remains constant is change. Despite our wish to freeze cherished moments in time, we find that treasured time is fleeting. It slips through our fingers; and before we have even stopped kissing the dimples in our infant's chubby hands, those hands are gripping bicycle handlebars, schoolbooks, telephones, and steering wheels.

We stand on porches and in airports, bidding loved ones good-bye as they leave for independent lives of their own. Tears are shed, love is expressed, and hugs are held longer than usual.

Painful as it is at times to bid a brief good-bye, we know change is good and essential for growth and progress. If a plant is not green, it is not growing. So, too, with mankind; if we stay in the same, familiar surroundings—never venturing out to stretch our wings in a new direction—we do not grow.

And though we miss our loved ones when they leave, a part of us celebrates their independence and the excitement of their next adventure. By keeping in touch, by sharing those new experiences, we discover that our own souls expand along with theirs. We find that we had nothing to fear, after all, for the most important part of a relationship—its love—remains strong and true despite a separation.

We discover that change has, in fact, enriched our relationships. Each of us reunites with our loved ones with more to offer from the lessons we've learned, more to teach to those who have not ventured where we have.

We remember that without change there would be no brilliant butterflies where once drab caterpillars crawled; no laughter of grandchildren clamoring upon Grandpa's knee; no coral sunsets at the end of a perfect day.

Change is part of God's plan. It is essential for our growth and can be a welcome respite from the routine—a grand opportunity to reach and learn, to find happiness in unexpected places. When we bid good-bye, let us remember that parting is but another opportunity to find significant growth and a deeper love.

· C H O I C E ·

Free to Choose

TRULY, IF THERE IS ANYTHING worse than suffering the consequences of our own bad decisions, it is watching those we love choose unwisely. Consider for a moment the plight of that tragic Shakespearean figure King Lear. After dividing up his kingdom among his daughters and their husbands, he is forced to watch them make one disastrous decision after another, ultimately bringing both country and family to the brink of ruin. He cries in helpless rage to the skies above, when he realizes that he cannot stop them.

We need not be kings to share Lear's royal grief. One modern mother's reaction is representative. After helping her much-loved son navigate his way through childhood and adolescence, she now finds herself grounded while watching him try out the wings of young adulthood for himself. She wisely understands that this is the natural course of things, but the experience is painful nonetheless, for, although her son has been well taught, he is not currently making the kinds of choices that will bring him lasting satisfaction. On occasion, this mother has been known to joke ruefully that only *other* people's children should have the right to make up their own minds.

Of course, grown children are not the only ones who cause

27

us concern. Who among us has not experienced frustration and even sorrow as we watch a spouse or a friend or a parent make a decision that may lead to future unhappiness. Indeed, if we had our own way, most of us would actively prevent them from doing so. We would keep them safely pastured, free from all harm and evil, forever in a watchful shepherd's sight.

And yet, as those who have been without it can attest, the freedom to choose is one of life's finest blessings. When we make choices, we are giving expressions to who we are and what we value the most. When we make choices, good or bad, we are able to learn something about ourselves and the world around us.

When we make choices, we are exercising the God-given gift of agency. To deny another adult this privilege is wrong. We cannot choose for other people, no matter how good our intentions may be. Each one of us must be free to decide for ourselves and to accept the consequences that follow. It is in this way that we as human beings grow, becoming, in the process, profoundly rich in experience and in wisdom.

"Know This, That Every Soul Is Free"

KNOW THIS, THAT EV'RY SOUL IS FREE to choose his life and what he'll be."[1] These stirring words remind us all of what a marvelous thing agency is. What greater blessing could there be, after all, than the opportunity to make decisions affecting our own destinies: who our friends will be, where we will live, what line of work we will pursue!

And yet, it must be admitted that there are times when this very same gift feels like more of a burden than a blessing. In today's sophisticated world, made ever smaller by continued advances in transportation and telecommunications, there is often an amazing array of choices: produce bins at the local market overflow with apples shipped from all over the world; clothing racks in department stores are filled with a hundred varieties of white shirts; commercials on television scream the advantages of one long-distance phone company over all the rest. So many options in so many areas of our lives can leave us feeling confused and overwhelmed.

Making choices under such circumstances becomes even more difficult when we want to make the *right* one.

"Choose the right," the old hymn exhorts, "when a choice is placed before you!"[2] But how do we know which choice is the right one for us? Sometimes, the challenge of making a decision becomes too much, and we respond simply by making no choice at all—paralyzed by indecision.

When we feel like this, it is helpful to remember that some of the decisions we make on a daily basis are not crucial. Similarly, many of our daily choices are not between right and wrong, good and evil—but between two rights, two good things. Realizing this can free us from the pressure of making the "perfect" decision.

There are times, however, when we do, in fact, choose poorly. We make bad decisions and commit errors in judgment. At those moments when we are confronted by the unhappy consequences of our choices, it is important to remember that there is recovery from our mistakes. We can stop; we can evaluate; we can make adjustments; we can go on, hopefully the wiser for our experience. And most comforting, we can be forgiven by the One who, in the words of Martin Luther, "overcometh all."[3]

1. Author unknown (ca. 1805), "Know This, That Every Soul Is Free," *Hymns of The Church of Jesus Christ of Latter-day Saints* (Salt Lake City: The Church of Jesus Christ of Latter-day Saints, 1985), no. 240.

2. Joseph L. Townsend, "Choose the Right," *Hymns of The Church of Jesus Christ of Latter-day Saints*, no. 239.

3. Martin Luther, "A Mighty Fortress," *Hymns of The Church of Jesus Christ of Latter-day Saints*, no. 68.

· COMPASSION ·

"Blessed Are They Who Comfort"

Blessed are they who comfort. Whether in death, disease, or despair, sweet relief can come from kind people who make efforts to ease the grief or trouble of others. A compassionate touch, a thoughtful note, a listening ear, or even a lighthearted diversion gives strength and hope to those who suffer.

We may recognize the need for comfort but not know how to give it. Perhaps we're uncertain about what to say or do when others are hurting. Each of us has struggled to find the right words, the best gesture, the most meaningful token. We wish we could explain the inexplicable, repair shattered hearts, and restore justice. But sometimes the best we can do is just be there to share the sorrow.

One woman suggests that comfort is found in companionship. She explains: "Maybe we have to learn that often there is no 'solution' for suffering. Everyone has some of it, sooner or later. What helps is to have one or two people around who keep trying to understand, who are willing to just hold our hand as we walk through it."[1] All of which require sensitivity and good judgment. Sometimes heartache becomes more bearable when we can talk about it. And other times, a warm embrace is reassuring.

Or as a father recalls, a well-timed outing can be consoling.

The burden of his young son's death was eased when a friend took him for a ride in his convertible. The sun showered them with warmth. The wind wiped away his tears. The hum of the car drowned out his sorrows for a moment in time. They didn't talk much, but somehow his suffering had been shared. He felt a healing begin to take place.

But where can we turn when our sorrow cannot be shared, when we find ourselves without a companion? The Lord, who suffered for all, assures us that we will never be left alone: "I will not leave you comfortless: I will come to you."[2] Ironically, we usually find Him and His promised peace while looking out for others in need of comfort.

1. Catharine Maurica, *Let Me Hear Your Voice* (New York City: Fawcett Columbine, 1993), 162.
2. *New Testament,* John 14:18.

Mourning with Those Who Mourn

ONE SURE MEASUREMENT of the stature of our souls is how we respond to those around us who are struggling to endure life's challenges. We will each experience grief and failure, loneliness and discouragement, but true compassion requires us to look past our own needs and help others—to mourn with those who mourn and comfort those who need comfort.[1]

None is immune to life's sorrows. Even the Old Testament prophet Elijah—who was taken to heaven in a fiery chariot—endured rejection, felt depression, and experienced times like we all do when life's "journey is too great" for us to go on without the intervention of God and others.[2]

Our willingness to mourn with those who mourn demonstrates that we understand that we're all fellow travelers, walking at different points on the same rocky path of mortality. During our difficult moments and life's soul-stretching cycles, each of us determines whether our personal trials will leave us bitter or make us better.

Truly great people allow their own past suffering to fill them with compassion for others. During some of the most trying events of his life, one who suffered much wrote, "It seems to me that my heart will always be more tender after this."[3] The essence of life is learning to valiantly endure our own trials, while helping others do the same.

The Bible's shortest verse says simply, "Jesus wept." Standing at the gravesite beside Lazarus' grieving sisters, the Master shared their grief—mourning with those who mourned in spite of His knowledge that Lazarus would be raised from the dead.[4]

Our willingness to mourn with those who mourn and to ease the suffering of others may be the truest definition for compassion. We can share others' grief and their burdens even when we can't entirely eliminate them. The family and friends of one recently diagnosed cancer patient have not tried to do what medicine must; instead of a cure, they have offered companionship, loving compassion, and the promise that the horrors of cancer and its treatment will not be faced alone.

God has not abandoned the meek, disregarded the grief-stricken, or forgotten those who mourn; but often He seeks to bless and comfort them through us. When our hearts become full of compassion, then God's love can reach down from above through us and carry us all closer to our heavenly home.

---

1. *Book of Mormon*, Mosiah 18:9.

2. *Old Testament*, 1 Kings 19:4–7.

3. *History of The Church of Jesus Christ of Latter-day Saints*, 7 vols., ed. B. H. Roberts (Salt Lake City: Deseret Book Company, 1970), 3:285–86. (Joseph Smith Jr.'s letter to Mrs. Norman Bull, written from Liberty Jail on March 15, 1839.)

4. *New Testament*, John 11:35–44.

Purposeful Praise

T HERE IS POWER IN THE PRINCIPLE of praise that can have a profound effect on how we perceive not only ourselves but also all the world around us.

Hollow expressions are not what constitute praise. Rather, praise in its purest sense suggests recognizing that which is good and then giving others the credit they're due. What parent has not heaped much-needed encouragement upon children who, for the first time, have attempted something beyond their normal capacity? And how many of us have benefitted from friends who have been thoughtful enough to offer an extra measure of support?

As we look for what we might praise in another, a story from the life of the Irish poet Thomas Moore provides insight. Upon returning home from a lengthy trip, he found that his beautiful bride had been stricken with smallpox and had locked herself in her room so that he would not see her scarred and pocked face. Rather than be deterred by her pleadings that he never look upon her again, he spent the night composing a song that he sang to her through the door the next morning. Contained in the verses he penned was his promise that, though her "endearing young charms" might fade, he would always find within her those qualities that were most worth recognizing.[1]

Perhaps this provides a pattern for all of us to follow as we choose what to sincerely commend in others. We will then find our views echoing those of the Psalmist, who spoke concerning the nature of men and women in these words: "For thou hast made [them] a little lower than the angels, and hast crowned [them] with glory and honour."[2] Sharing such a view with Him who created mankind certainly will bring into clearer focus the potential within each of us that is worthy of praise.

Praise that reflects the goodness inherent in all mankind is never fleeting and always supportive.

---

1. Howard W. Hunter, *The Teachings of Howard W. Hunter*, ed. Clyde J. Williams (Salt Lake City; Bookcraft, 1997), 134–35.
2. *Old Testament*, Psalm 8:5.

Time Enough for Courtesy

FOR THE PAST FEW MONTHS, the fierce winter weather has battered much of the world. Brutal ice storms have glazed highways and byways, making travel dangerous. Heavy snowstorms have forced businesses to shut down early and sometimes altogether. Cruel cold has caused pipes to freeze and even the closure of schools on occasion.

Such conditions certainly complicate everyday life. Buses, commuter trains, and airplanes operate behind schedule. Hardware stores run low on essential supplies, such as salt and snow shovels. Letters arrive later than usual. Outings and activities are cancelled again and again.

In the face of such complications, people understandably feel out of sorts. They turn testy and often respond to one another out of irritation—honking the car horn a little too quickly at an intersection, speaking abruptly with store clerks, snapping at family members.

One young mother recently found herself becoming grumpier by the moment as she tried to negotiate a stroller with her infant son through a parking lot filled with ice and huge mounds of snow. When she finally reached the entrance of the store, people bumped and jostled past, letting the heavy doors slam shut before she and her baby could get through. The mother thought she might scream in sheer frustration, when suddenly a large, rather rough-looking man stepped in front of her.

"You look like you need an extra set of hands," he said, holding the door open wide as she wheeled her baby into the warmth of the store. When she thanked him, he merely shrugged and said: "We all have to help each other out."

Ralph Waldo Emerson observed that "life is not so short but that there is always time enough for courtesy."[1] Simply put, courtesy is a basic respect and consideration for others, no matter what the situation. Indeed, the more stressful the situation, the greater the need for courtesy. Small, thoughtful deeds, such as remembering to say "thank you," standing aside to let someone else pass, or holding a door open, can go a long way toward easing the inevitable tensions of daily life.

Acts such as these are always welcome—as welcome, in fact, as sun on a winter's day.

---

1. Ralph Waldo Emerson, in *Bartlett's Familiar Quotations,* 15th edition, ed. John Bartlett (Boston: Little, Brown and Company, 1980), 499.

"Though Deepening Trials": When There Are No Answers

IN TODAY'S PROGRAM SELECTION "Though Deepening Trials," there is the recognition that, at one time or another, tribulation comes to us all. Whether young or old, rich or poor, male or female, we cannot entirely avoid trouble. We cannot, in the memorable words of Hamlet, miss those "slings and arrows of outrageous fortune."[1]

If there is anything more difficult than dealing with adversity ourselves, however, it may be having to witness the people we care about wrestle with their own set of personal problems. Who among us has not experienced the pain of watching a much-loved child face rejection by his peers? Who has not ached for an elderly family member dealing with declining health? Who has not tasted the grief of a grief-stricken friend?

During times of trouble, our natural tendency is to ask why. Why do bad things happen to the people we love? Why must they suffer? And, as human beings, we like answers. We expect answers. We find comfort in answers.

One woman remembers the time her daughter and son-in-law lost the child they were joyously expecting in the seventh month of pregnancy. Naturally, the shock she and everyone close to the young couple felt was profound. Everything had appeared to be completely normal. Even the doctor was surprised by the unexpected turn of events. What, then, had gone wrong? And why should such a thing happen to her daughter and her husband, both of whom desperately wanted a child?

The woman's first impulse was to approach the couple with comforting answers—the kind of answers well-intentioned people often give in times of sorrow: maybe this was a part of heaven's plan for them; maybe Heaven had chosen to call this baby home.

The daughter listened sadly, then said: "Maybe we just don't know what the answers are."

The woman realized that her comments had actually sounded like platitudes, meant to gloss over another's grief; and at that moment, the thought occurred to her that, where there can be no answers, there can always be love—the kind of love that enfolds us in its arms and whispers, "I am so sorry for your pain."

It is this kind of answer, sympathetic and accepting of life's mysteries, that can truly give comfort and perhaps help those who are suffering to find a measure of peace.

---

1. William Shakespeare, *Hamlet,* act III, scene i, line 58, *The Complete Works of Shakespeare* (New York City: Doubleday and Company, Inc., 1936), 752.

· COURAGE ·

Silhouettes of Courage

T HERE ARE TWO KINDS OF COURAGE. There is the bravery to take risks, to fight wars, to plunge into an icy river to save someone else from drowning. Daring heroes and valiant military generals come to mind. Most of us stand in awe of such.

But there is also another quiet kind of courage, which is often overlooked. It is the courage to hold back.

When Jackie Robinson became the first man of his race to play professional baseball, he made history. The president of the Brooklyn Dodgers asked Jackie if he had the courage to play the game despite the racial persecution they both knew lay ahead.

Jackie asked if he was looking for a black man who was afraid to fight. The president replied that he was looking for a ballplayer with the courage *not* to fight.[1]

Jackie did have that courage. Only by exercising tremendous restraint, when others might have given in to anger, was he able to open a door of equality and open the eyes of the world to the real meaning of courage. People all over the globe saw a courageous Jackie Robinson play baseball. But only those behind the scenes saw an even larger hero—the hero who held back.

How often are we tempted to leap ahead, to follow passions and impulses, forgetting the courage it takes to remain silent, to make sacrifices, to ignore opportunities to get even. Sometimes, courage shines brightest when we forgive another or when we admit we were wrong.

Désiré Joseph Cardinal Mercier reminds us that "it needs courage to throw oneself forward, but it needs not less to hold oneself back."[2] Our daily lives are filled with opportunities to show the kind of quiet courage that resists temptation.

We see courage in those who struggle with adversity, refusing to give in to bitterness or blame. Discovering that they cannot change poor health or the loss of a loved one, courageous people change their outlooks and find they can rise above personal tragedy and even give to others.

The single mother who raises her children all alone, the man who faces ridicule and scorn for his honesty at work, the family that pulls together when faced with financial setbacks—all are valiant soldiers in a battle. The battle may not be a public one, but it requires no less courage.

Wrote Robert Louis Stevenson, "Yours is not the less noble because no drum beats before you when you go out into your daily battlefields, and no crowds shout about your coming when you return from your daily victory or defeat."[3]

And yet, by choosing carefully, by pausing to reflect, by taking the higher path even when it is difficult, we can all be heroes—great silhouettes of courage on the battlefield of life.

---

1. Spencer Johnson, *The Value of Courage: The Story of Jackie Robinson* (La Jolla, California: Value Communications, Inc., 1977), 35.

2. Edward F. Murphy, ed., *The Crown Treasury of Relevant Quotations* (New York City: Crown Publishers, Inc.,1978), 188.

3. William Safire and Leonard Safire, eds., *Words of Wisdom* (New York City: Simon & Schuster, 1989), 76.

"Be Not Afraid"

ON THE MOST MEMORABLE SUNDAY in history,[1] Mary Magdalene and other women set out at dawn for the Lord's tomb. Upon arriving, they were consoled by an angel: "Fear not ye: for I know that ye seek Jesus."[2] And then, a little later, the Lord himself comforted, "Be not afraid."[3]

These gentle and powerful assurances of Easter morning are especially meaningful in our world today. When the headlines are filled with tragedy and violence—when we live with uncertainties and wrestle with change almost every day—fear could easily overwhelm us. Without question, much of life can be unsettling. But the Savior's life and teachings show us the way to "be not afraid."

Not long ago, a woman became upset after viewing a news magazine program. She began to worry and wonder. The images of disease and suffering troubled her to the point of sleeplessness. Wanting to dismiss these negative thoughts, she knelt by her bed and prayed. She sought for wisdom and perspective, and before long, peace filled her heart. She was able to think more clearly and to decide upon some protective measures for herself and family. The scripture came to mind: "For God hath not given us the spirit of fear; but of power, and of love, and of a sound mind."[4]

In this way, fear can actually teach us. Eleanor Roosevelt wrote: "You gain strength, courage and confidence by every experience in which you really stop to look fear in the face. You are able to say to yourself, I lived through this . . . I can take the next thing that comes along."[5] Whether as a child, a youth, or an adult, when we work through our fears and enlist the Lord's help in overcoming them, we discover strength we didn't know we had. The things, or even the people we fear may not change, but we grow in our ability to manage and understand them.

While fear is normal in times of distress, it need not remain with us and keep us from living and loving with a fullness of heart.

The Lord has comforted His children all through the ages: "Be strong and of a good courage; be not afraid, neither be thou dismayed: for the Lord thy God is with thee."[6]

1. James E. Talmage, *Jesus the Christ* (Salt Lake City: Deseret Book Company, 1970), 678.
2. *New Testament,* Matthew 28:5.
3. *New Testament,* Matthew 28:10.
4. *New Testament,* 2 Timothy 1:7.
5. "You Learn by Living," in *Bartlett's Book of Quotations* (Boston: Little, Brown & Company, 1992), 654.
6. *Old Testament,* Joshua 1:9.

Heroism

HEROES COME IN MANY FORMS, and heroic acts occur in many settings and situations. A hero is one who reaches inside oneself and manages to reach beyond personal limitations, fears, and difficulties. We honor those heroes of our shared past—those who offered their lives as a shield against tyranny and oppression. We honor those who died and also those who lived, whose minds or spirits or bodies may be forever scarred by the horrors of warfare and violence. We also honor those heroes among us who show us that the need for commitment and sacrifice has not vanished.

We honor those rare individuals whose deeds ring out in the cause of preserving freedom. From the patriotic heroism of soldiers fighting in foreign lands or keeping peace across the world today, we learn indelible lessons of courage and sacrifice.

We honor as well the everyday heroism of parents fighting daily battles against drugs and hopelessness, the heroism of firefighters and officers of the law who risk their lives to protect us, the heroism of missionaries across the globe who serve tirelessly to bring a message of hope and peace to lands where these are rare commodities. The world has many heroes—and many kinds of heroes. From all our heroes we learn of commitment and the strength that come from within.

When life becomes difficult or dangerous—when our resources seem stretched to the breaking point—we can find within us resources of extraordinary fortitude and faith. The goods of heroism are within us all. May we allow courage and honor to define our response to whatever tribulations we may face. May we, too, become heroes.

· DEATH ·

"If a Man Die, Shall He Live Again?"

Who among us has not mourned at the death of a loved one? Death is no respecter of persons—it claims rich and poor, strong and weak, saint and sinner alike. Death snuffs the flickering candle of old age and stills the joyful laughter of children.

Whether a loved one's death is unexpected or anticipated, sudden or after years of suffering, it is death's finality that fills our hearts with feelings of grief, regret, uncertainty, and sorrow. In the long and empty hours that follow the death of a loved one, we are repeatedly confronted by the age-old question uttered by Job: "If a man die, shall he live again?"[1]

While death is inevitable, our reaction to it is a matter of choice. We can live out our days trembling in the shadow of death, or we can choose to be illuminated by the all-encompassing hope that shines from the Lord's empty tomb. As we trust in Him, our feelings of helplessness and despair can melt away as we exercise faith in His promise: "I am the resurrection, and the life: he that believeth in me, though he were dead, yet shall he live."[2]

The legacy of the empty tomb is the promise that we, too, shall live again. While death is one of the most difficult parts of life, it can also be one of the most beautiful and sacred: beautiful because with it comes the hope of the resurrection; sacred because, while we mourn for the moment, death allows us to look forward with an eye of faith to the day foretold in scripture when "God shall wipe away all tears from their eyes; and there shall be no more death, neither sorrow, nor crying, neither shall there be any more pain: for the former things are passed away."[3]

When we choose to live in the light of the empty tomb, we speak less of bitterness and more of understanding, less of emptiness and more of empathy, less of loss and more of reunion, less of tragedy and more of destiny. It is not oblivion, but destiny that awaits us beyond death's darkened door. And, trusting in God that one day He will reunite us with those we love and cherish, we can rejoice in the truth reflected by the words of William W. Phelps:

> There is no end to glory;
> There is no end to love;
> There is no end to being;
> There is no death above.[4]

1. *Old Testament,* Job 14:14.
2. *New Testament,* John 11:25.
3. *New Testament,* Revelation 21:4.
4. William W. Phelps, "If You Could Hie to Kolob," *Hymns of The Church of Jesus Christ of Latter-day Saints* (Salt Lake City: The Church of Jesus Christ of Latter-day Saints, 1985), no. 284.

The Beauty of the Requiem

FOR MOST OF US, THE OCCASIONS are rare when we're led to think about death and recognize our own mortality. Yet, from time to time you and I need to ponder the subject; in particular, we need to honor the memory of valiant men and women who've given their lives to establish and preserve the blessings we cherish in our nation.

When we remember our heroes, we open a window of introspection and we see more clearly our own divine nature and purpose. Our vision becomes especially vivid when music provides a setting for reflections on death.

In a modern composition titled *An American Requiem,* James DeMars created what he calls "a sense of empathy that one extends to whoever suffered a loss." Webster defines requiem as "a musical composition in honor of the dead," and DeMars said that, while composing the Requiem, he often had in mind a "picture of the funeral service of John F. Kennedy.

"It was the first time I had seen a funeral of state in the grand sense of a nation mourning the loss of a president," DeMars said.

What pictures flashed through your mind the last time you attended a funeral? What did you think as speakers recalled the accomplishments and virtues of a friend or family member? Did you wonder what others will say about you when you die? Did you develop a new sense of purpose and resolve?

One woman said, "As I sat listening at the funeral of an elderly man I had known only a short time, I was surprised to discover the rich, full life of caring and service he had given during his years of health and productivity. I was overcome with a desire to follow his example and give more of myself to my family, my neighbors, and my community."

James DeMars expressed similar sentiments. Through his music—his Requiem—DeMars said he hopes the listeners will realize that "the best way to honor and remember the ones we've lost is to live the best possible life we can, [knowing] that we're sheltered by the grace of God and [that we can] dignify our existence with good living."

And so, we learn a truism: that by honoring the dead, we inspire and motivate the living. As Lincoln said, "From these honored dead we take increased devotion to that cause for which they gave the last full measure of devotion . . . [and] highly resolve that these dead shall not have died in vain."[1]

---

1. Abraham Lincoln, in *Bartlett's Familiar Quotations*, 15th edition, ed. John Bartlett (Boston: Little, Brown, and Company, 1980), 523.
   Quotes by James DeMars were taken from the transcript of his recorded conversation in December 1993.

The Joy of Going Home

AFTER THREE LONG YEARS of living in a foreign land, a young woman was finally on her way back home. As her plane approached the shores of her home, her tears could not be restrained. She was filled with an enormous feeling of love for all her family, who were anticipating her return. All she could think of was home and what a joyful reunion it would be to be with her parents and other family members again.

Thirty-five years later, this same woman sat at the bedside of her eighty-nine-year-old widowed mother, who was dying—a mother who had longed for several years to be with her beloved husband and other family members who had gone to "the other side." The daughter realized it was now her mother's turn to be "going home." Having experienced the joyful feelings that going home can bring, she was able to let her mother go; and through her sorrow, she felt a sweet peace and happiness for her mother. Leonardo da Vinci once said, "As a well-spent day brings happy sleep, so life well used brings happy death."[1] The peace this daughter felt emanated from her knowledge that her mother had lived a life of service and caring, and many who benefitted from that caring were waiting to greet her.

Each one of us on this earth will one day be going home to that heavenly place where a loving Father in Heaven and family members await us. It is all part of a divine plan. "We come [to this earth] not by accident or chance, but as part of a glorious everlasting plan."[2] What we do while we are here determines how joyful our going home will be.

As loved ones gather around a family member nearing the end of his or her life, there is a sadness; and yet, when that person has lived a life of goodness, there is a sweetness that prevails. Stories are shared and loving memories relived. It is a tender scene. And what might we see if our eyes could behold the gathering of those on the other side? Surely, we would see loved ones preparing with excited anticipation for the long-awaited homecoming. Perhaps they, too, share precious memories of their loved one as the time draws near.

Think of it—surrounded by loved ones on both sides! Of such an occasion, Charles Frohman said, "It is the most beautiful adventure of life."[3] The composer of the song known by so many summed it up best when he wrote, "Lastin' joy now begun, For I'm goin' home."[4]

1. Leonardo da Vinci, in *LDS Collectors Library: 12,000 Famous Quotes*, CD-ROM (Salt Lake City: Infobases, Inc., 1995).
2. Richard L. Evans, in *Man's Search for Happiness*, videocassette (Salt Lake City: The Church of Jesus Christ of Latter-day Saints).
3. Charles Frohman, in *12,000 Famous Quotes*.
4. William Arms Fisher, "Goin' Home," sung to Antonín Dvořák's music based on the Largo from the *New World Symphony*.

"He Is Risen"

T HE INEVITABILITY OF LIFE IS DEATH. No matter what efforts we may make to avoid it, we each will eventually face this final moment of mortality.

And before that moment comes, most of us will experience the loss of one we love. Perhaps we have already stood over the grave of a spouse, a child taken in the flower of youth, a friend whose void we will never fill. And, in such moments, who has not asked, with Job, "If a man die, shall he live again?"[1]

That such a question could be answered in the affirmative may seem more a miracle than one could ever hope for. Yet, in addition to asking, Job also answered the great question of life when he declared: "I know that my redeemer liveth, . . . And though after my skin worms destroy this body, . . . in my flesh shall I see God."[2]

Such is the promise of the Resurrection—an event so transcendent, a miracle remembered throughout Christendom this Easter Sunday.

It seems appropriate that this day of hope be celebrated in the season of spring—as the brown hills of winter are turning again to vibrant green and as seeds, long dormant, are bringing forth blossoms that remind us yet again of the miraculous renewal and rebirth of all living things.

Gordon B. Hinckley said of the Resurrection: "As surely as there [has] been mortal death, there will be immortal life; and as certainly as there [has] been separation, there will be reunion. This is the faith which comes of Christ, who brought to all the promise of immortality."[3]

With this promise comes the assurance that each one of us born into this mortal realm will one day receive the blessings of an immortal soul, as our spirit and body are reunited through the miracle of the Resurrection. And combined with this miracle is the even greater gift given to all who seek to know the will of God and who then strive to live by His words—the promise of His atonement and the richness of eternal life.

Such are the miracles attested to by a solitary angel, who stood before an empty tomb and declared of the Savior of mankind, "He is risen; he is not here."[4]

47

1. *Old Testament,* Job 14:14.
2. *Old Testament,* Job 19:25–26.
3. Gordon B. Hinckley, "The Victory over Death," *Ensign,* May 1985, 51.
4. *New Testament,* Mark 16:6.

· FAITH ·

Where Can We Find God?

WHERE CAN WE FIND GOD? Where is He to be found? Amidst the rubble and fire of an earthquake, in the whipping wind of a hurricane, through the noisy destruction of war, dazed survivors look heavenward and in anguished cries ask the great questions: Where? Where can we find God? Where is He to be found?

To some, their gaze turns downward in hopelessness; it is a question without an answer. But others, searching skyward, can testify that God can be found. He is with us in the most unexpected places, under the most trying of circumstances.

The courage and hope of Anne Frank's diary reminds us that He can be found in a small attic, hidden carefully above an office; the bravery and faith of Zlata Filipovic's journal testifies that He walks through the shell-pitted streets of Sarajevo. Albert Einstein found Him in the nucleus of the atom, while Stephen Hawking searches for Him in the furthest reaches of the stars. He spoke to Alexander Solzhenitsyn in the cold, dark loneliness of a Siberian labor camp. And God ministered to the ill and starving poor of Calcutta through an elderly nun named Teresa.

God can be found in a friend's loving counsel, a word of encouragement, in a handclasp and a smile. God can be found in a classroom, a boardroom, or a prison. God can be found on a highway—in a stranger changing our flat tire. Or God can be found at home.

To many of us, God speaks through scribbled papers, lovingly displayed on a refrigerator door. God dwells in families and communities—wherever two or three are gathered in His name. And, as Elie Wiesel reminds us, "A child always suggests the presence of God."[1] Perhaps nowhere is He closer than in the trusting eyes and loving embraces of small children.

Where can we find God? Where is He to be found? In the heart that is pure, in the soul that longs for His comfort. In earthquakes and hurricanes and war itself—in quiet repose and noisy tumult—God is where we seek Him.

---

1. Henry James Cargas, *Conversations with Elie Wiesel* (South Bend, Indiana: Justice Books, 1992), 103.

Acts of Faith

ONE BRIGHT DAY IN OCTOBER, the autumn sunlight glancing off trees, a young mother put her three small children in the car and headed for the local garden center to buy daffodil bulbs. She thought it would be great fun for the children to help her tuck them deep in the earth, then wait for them to bloom in the spring.

The experience did not turn out exactly as she had hoped it would.

The children were far more interested in the candy bars at the checkout stand than in bulbs, which the mother herself had to admit resembled stray onions in the back of the family pantry. Even after the bulbs were purchased and taken home, the children weren't very enthusiastic about planting them once they learned it would be months before the daffodils actually bloomed. "How boring," they seemed to say, "a hobby that makes you wait!"

Discouraged, the mother told her husband that night that planting a bulb was a small but risky act of faith. "For one thing," she said, "you have to wait forever to see any results. For another, there may never be any results to see." After all, bulbs have been known not to flower.

Months later, on a late morning in March, one of the children burst through the front door screaming with delight at what she had just seen!

The mother stepped onto the front porch and saw it—the first of the daffodils curling its yellow lion's head over a cluster of small violets.

Planting a bulb in the autumn and waiting for it to bloom in the spring is like many other activities: buying winter sweaters on sale in July, planning for next year's vacation, storing one child's pair of Sunday shoes until his younger brother is big enough to wear them, sensing the return of summer in a winter's sun, loving someone today with the hope that love will be remembered tomorrow.

All of which require faith. Bulbs of belief, hope, and trust must be planted deep within our hearts, watered with patience, and nurtured by the Light of the World. Only then can we rejoice in the blossoms or blessings of life.

"Consider the Lilies of the Field"

ONE OF THE BEST WAYS TO FIND lasting peace in our ever-changing world is to take time to examine and enjoy earth's natural beauty. When life's tedious tasks and daily pressures weigh heavily upon us, important perspective can be gained by gazing at the night sky, examining a flower, or using a finger to trace the veins of a leaf.

When we look at nature, we see so much more than scenery. As poet Elizabeth Barrett Browning observed, "Earth's crammed with heaven, and every common bush afire with God; but only he who sees takes off his shoes."[1] Even nature's most ordinary scenes can teach and inspire us if we will but pause to observe them. Yet, far too often earth's natural beauty goes unnoticed because it is too close and too constant to command our attention. In the words of Emerson, "If the stars should appear one night in a thousand years, how would men believe and adore; and preserve for many generations the remembrance of the city of God which had been shown!"[2]

If, as poets and prophets have observed, "all things denote there is a God,"[3] then the way we look at the earth—and the plants, animals, and people who populate it—defines our relationship with deity. When we consider the lilies of the field, we are not only learning about nature, but we are also learning about ourselves. For, like the leaves, the clouds, and the stars, there are changing seasons and constant patterns in our own lives.

When we walk through life daily considering the lilies of the field, God is near—His name written in the sparkling stars, His love reflected by the morning dew, and His presence whispered with the rustle of autumn leaves. Our appreciation of nature is the most complete when we recognize the hand of the Divine Creator in His masterpieces that fill every meadow, every river, and every mountain.

By observing nature's shifting scenes, we learn that when life gives us winter or shadow or wind, it is also offering us the chance to become men and women with faith for all seasons. Though sometimes wearied and worn, we can learn to see beyond the wind and the weather and glimpse in nature the Creator of all things.

1. Elizabeth Barrett Browning, *Aurora Leigh,* book 7, lines 821–23 (Athens: Ohio University, 1992), 487.
2. Ralph Waldo Emerson, *The Works of Ralph Waldo Emerson* (Boston: Houghton, Mifflin and Company, 1883), 1:13.
3. *New Testament,* Ephesians 3:9; *The Book of Mormon,* Alma 30:44.

"I Will Lift Up Mine Eyes"

ON A STARLIT NIGHT, AWAY FROM the lights of the city, we can see a spectacular display in the heavens: stars without number—both dim and blazing brightly—patterns and guideposts that have inspired civilizations for centuries. Many are those who have looked into the nighttime sky and wondered about our relationship to the universe and what lies beyond this world.

After reflecting upon such things, one man wrote: "What is man's wisdom in comparison to [the universe]?"[1]

That question, asked in myriad forms over thousands of years, has spawned countless answers ranging from a determination to live by one's own wits to a resolute devotion to find and follow higher principles and purposes.

Surveys and studies suggest that most of us living today do, indeed, seek for—and find—meaning beyond our finite view of the world we see.

Such beliefs provided comfort to the Psalmist, who wrote that "God is known . . . for a refuge."[2] We often seek for that refuge through prayer, through meditating upon our lives and those teachings we feel impressed to follow, as well as through calling upon powers that exceed our own.

Though "prayer is and remains always a native and deepest impulse of the soul of man,"[3] wrote Thomas Carlyle, we sometimes fail to seek for or listen to what has been described as the "still small voice." Perhaps the noise of a far too busy world gets in the way—just as bright lights can obscure the sky—or maybe we have become so reliant on ourselves that we fail to respond to this most basic impulse.

Whatever the cause, when we fail to lift our eyes and our thoughts heavenward, we lose the opportunity to benefit from the quiet counsel and assurances promised us by a loving God. And day to day, our lives may thereby stray from the path we want and know we ought to follow.

The Psalmist continues: "I will lift up mine eyes unto the hills, from whence cometh my help. My help cometh from the Lord, which made heaven and earth."[4]

We need not feel alone in this world; we need not feel left to our own devices. Whether we are facing what seem like insurmountable obstacles or whether we are simply seeking greater peace for our soul, prayer can connect us to those powers that made both heaven and earth—and that will provide a refuge for us all.

1. John Taylor, *The Gospel Kingdom* (Salt Lake City: Bookcraft, 1987), 17.
2. *Old Testament*, Psalm 48:3.
3. Thomas Carlyle, in *Webster's New World Dictionary of Quotable Definitions*, ed. Eugene E. Brussel (Englewood Cliffs, New Jersey: Prentice Hall, 1988), 448.
4. *Old Testament*, Psalm 121:1–2.

Touched by the Hands of His Love

SOMETIMES, WHEN WE ARE CAUGHT UP in meeting the many demands of life, our vision narrows and we fail to see God's gifts of goodness and mercy. Because we are all His children and He cares about us deeply, we experience times when we are touched by the hands of His love.

One winter day, a businessman had such an experience. He

discovered that his favorite pen—one he had carried for years—was missing. He searched everywhere and even offered a silent prayer to be able to find the treasured pen, but to no avail. The next morning he felt impressed to leave for work earlier than usual. After arriving at his destination, he stepped out of his car into the rain and, to his surprise, there, lying in a puddle of water was his pen. He could hardly believe his good fortune. In a matter of minutes, the rain turned to snow and he realized that, had he not left early that morning, his pen would have been hidden beneath a blanket of snow. A coincidence? He didn't think so. That day he knew he had been touched by the hands of God's love.

One woman reported she had been feeling frustrated and forsaken over a serious problem she was going through. That evening a friend called, saying: "I've been thinking about you and felt like I needed to call you. How are you doing?" With that invitation, the woman poured out her heart to her friend. She had received the best gift anyone can give in an hour of need—a listening ear. At that moment she, too, was touched by the hands of His love.

Another woman shared her sorrow over the failing mental capacity of her elderly mother. She longed for the days when she had been able to share her joys and sorrows with her. One day, when she desperately needed an encouraging word from her aged mother, a tiny miracle happened. For an instant, it was as though her mother were her loving self again. She put her arms around her daughter and whispered, "Everything will be all right, dear. I love you." Then, her mind was gone again. The daughter realized that a caring Father in Heaven knew her need and granted it, if only for a moment. And in that moment, they were both touched by the hands of His love.

When a loving word is whispered, when the sunlight sparkles on a lake, when a baby smiles, when a bird sings its song of promise, or when a simple prayer is answered, we need to notice. All of these and so many other wonders of life are witnesses that we have been touched by the hands of God's love.

· FAMILY ·

What Goes into a Home?

A WOMAN ACCUSTOMED TO AFFLUENCE once traveled to a foreign land. While there, she was invited into what most from her circumstances would have considered a mere hovel—a one-room dwelling with no running water, a single light bulb, and an open fire upon which the family cooked its meals.

Despite such conditions, the visitor later observed: "There was a special feeling there. The room was clean. The bare cement floor was spotless and . . . colorfully painted dishes lined the shelves. . . . Even though poor, [this family] had created an environment in which special warmth and goodness could grow and thrive."[1]

Despite the pressures we often feel to the contrary, a home is not made up of the possessions we spend so much of our energy pursuing. Rather, a home is built of relationships based on love, trust, and mutual support; as children learn from such examples; and as parents and children take time to play together, to talk one with another, to share in the many individual activities that sometimes can pull a family apart.

One young mother told of her own father—a well-known and overworked government official who stuck his head into her bedroom to say goodnight late one evening. As he asked her in passing how everything was going, he sensed that all was not well for his teenage daughter; so he went into her room, sat with her, and listened as she talked at length about all the problems she was facing at school and with her friends.

Though he probably could have justified leaving to attend to weightier matters—or simply to get the sleep he so sorely needed—he stayed with her and listened long into the night. "I don't really remember what he even said," the daughter later recalled, "except that he loved me and that I was a wonderful person—when I really wasn't . . . being the nicest person in the world to be around."[2]

Some of us, sadly, work unceasingly to pay for our homes and all that goes in them, forgetting as we do so that what goes on in our homes is far more important than what goes into our houses.

Perhaps, as we remember that love can abound in any abode, we will increasingly have as our foremost concern providing our families with an environment that will lift the souls of all who dwell therein.

1. Sherrie Johnson, *Spiritually Centered Motherhood* (Salt Lake City: Bookcraft, 1983), 81.
2. *BYU Today,* vol. 43, no. 4 (July 1989): 42.

The Worth of a Child

HAVE YOU HELD A NEWBORN BABY in your arms and, in wonder and reverence, asked yourself: "Who is this child that God has sent? Who will this innocent little soul become, and what great work has he or she been sent to do?" Every child is a gift from God to be honored, nurtured, and prepared for life's important purposes. We never know the influence for good we may have in the life of a child.

Did the young father and mother of a tiny baby named George Washington know, as they looked into his trusting eyes, that those very eyes would one day see the vision of democracy and lead a revolution that would establish a nation? Probably not. And yet, every ounce of faith and courage they exhibited and taught helped achieve such greatness. But first, he was just a child.

Consider the parents of Johann Sebastian Bach. Did they know how their musical influence would shape his life? Though they died when he was only ten years old, they had nurtured him well on his way to become one of the most revered composers of all time. And what of the influence of his older brother, Cristoph? Seeing the potential in his younger brother, Johann, he continued the task of helping him reach that potential. Now, the music of Bach inspires mankind in great halls, cathedrals, and homes throughout the world. But first, he was just a child.

Could the parents of Florence Nightingale have known that the child they held in their arms would one day almost single-handedly care for armies of wounded and dying soldiers? No. And yet, their influence on her education and social graces would prove valuable in a future they had no idea existed for her. Years after her death, she is known worldwide as the founder of today's nursing profession. But first, she was just a child.

We do not know if the child we read our bedtime stories to will become president of a nation, or if the child we teach a mathematical concept to will become a renowned scientist, or if the child we help to enjoy and appreciate the beauty of nature will become a great artist. However, this we do know: every minute spent in nurturing, playing with, and teaching children will help them accomplish God's great design for them here on earth. By nurturing a child, we nurture the future.

Love and Boundaries

To EXPERIENCE LOVE AT HOME is how we learn what love really is. One young adult woman was a witness to this truth when she said, "It was my parents who taught me how to love." She explained that they taught her by the way they treated each of their children—particularly her brother, when he was going through a rebellious stage of drinking and drugs. At times she couldn't see how her parents could keep on loving him when his attitude and actions were so negative and contrary to what he had been taught. She told how, when he turned eighteen, her parents said he could not live at home if he didn't obey their family rules of no drinking and no drugs, but that he was always welcome for a home-cooked meal and would be included in all family activities, regardless. They spoke to him in a kind, loving way but were firm about the rules. The boy chose to move out on his own. His parents would visit him and treat him normally, without criticism. He felt such love from them that he soon gave up his bad habits, returned home, and went on with his education.

There is nothing more powerful than that kind of love. One family therapist said that, to effectively set boundaries for children, parents need to be kind, gentle, respectful, and firm. He went on to explain, "If you leave out *kind, gentle,* and *respectful,* then *firm* won't have a leg to stand on."[1] It only creates bad feelings and drives children away. On the other hand, they cannot continue to resist love that comes wrapped in those virtues. Rules then become acceptable—even a confirmation of parental love.

A seventeen-year-old young man was taking his date to her door after returning from a school dance. When his girlfriend invited him to come in, he told her it was too late—that his parents insisted on his being home by a certain time and that he was not at all happy about it, but he knew he had to obey or they would come looking for him. She quietly said: "I would give anything to have parents who cared that much. Mine don't even know when I come home, and they couldn't care less. You're very lucky to have parents like that."

There has never been a time when the world was in greater need of parents caring enough to set boundaries by being kind, gentle, respectful, and firm. English author Maria Jane Jewsbury wrote, "The power to love truly and devotedly is the noblest gift with which a human being can be endowed."[2]

Children of today desperately need this kind of devoted love shown to them.

1. Gary B. Lundberg, *I Don't Have to Make Everything All Better* (Las Vegas, Nevada: Riverpark Publishing Company, 1995), 26, 213.
2. Maria Jane Jewsbury, in *The New Dictionary of Thoughts* (n.p.: Standard Book Company, 1961), 375.

A Mother's Prayer

Recently, a seven-year-old girl was taken ill. When her parents sought medical attention, they were told that, while her illness certainly was not life-threatening, it likely would leave her weak for quite some time. As the days passed, this girl's young mind could not comprehend why she continued to feel so sick. Then, one evening she hit upon an answer and told her mother, "Mommy, the reason I'm not getting better is because you're not praying for me." Somewhat chagrined, the mother replied, "Oh, but I am praying for you—every morning and every night—and so is Dad and each of your sisters." With that assurance, the little girl's spirits were lifted, which, in turn, helped her ward off her illness. And, of course, the mother made certain that her daughter was more aware of her family's daily prayers.

The song says, "Something of God is in a mother's love."[1]

Indeed, something of the divine does seem evident—first, as mothers bring children into the world, and then as they draw upon God's powers in lifting, teaching, and blessing their children. One mother's son told of the challenges and trials he had faced as a boy and how, in difficult moments, he would remember his widowed mother's sacrifices, her concern for his welfare, and her reliance upon her Heavenly Father as she raised him.

Then, he explained that "this feeling toward my mother became a defense, a barrier between me and temptation, so that I could turn aside from temptation and sin by . . . the love begotten in my soul toward her whom I knew loved me more than . . . any other living being."[2]

There is no doubt that the many demands of mothering can be trying, exhausting, and even painful at times. Teaching children who seem to have little interest in the lessons they need to learn can seem fruitless at the moment and may cause understandable consternation.

Yet, those mothers who see a connection between themselves and the divine are wise, indeed; they bring blessings upon themselves and their children as they pray for their children's well-being.

A mother filled with faith will have a powerful effect on her children's lives as she adds to her efforts a dimension that only God can give.

---

1. Grace Noll Crowell, "A Mother's Love," in *Songs of Faith* (New York City: Harper and Bros., 1994).

2. Joseph F. Smith, *Gospel Doctrine* (Salt Lake City: Deseret Book Company, 1919), 314–15.

The Title Most Noble

THROUGHOUT OUR LIVES WE ACQUIRE TITLES. Many come to us through our work—doctor, supervisor, senator, captain. Others come to us as members of a family—uncle, aunt, mom, dad.

Titles shape our identity and define our role not only for others around us but also for ourselves. And while many such labels spell prestige or success to some, too many forget one of the most important titles of all—one requiring more talent, greater responsibility, and more Godlike qualities—the title of father.

Nowhere else is your influence more needed than in your role as nurturer, teacher, and leader of the young ones entrusted to your care. In no other capacity are you truly irreplaceable.

Harold B. Lee once said that the most important work a man will ever do "will be the work you do within the walls of your own home."[1] A father who makes his family his top priority will work in tandem with his wife to rear capable children. They, in turn, will grow up feeling loved and secure—eager to do good in the world. It is the greatest work a man could ever find.

A quick glance at the troubles which beset our world reveals that many are traceable to the absence of a father in the home. Not only children—but all of society—need strong men who will teach correct principles to their young.

Conversely, many of our greatest leaders give credit to the father who put aside his work to be there at their ballgames, or made time just to talk, or wrestled or played with them. Fathers who spend time with their children make an investment for all of us: they give us well-adjusted, happy children who grow up to cure diseases, right wrongs, and make the world a better place.

One child development specialist challenged parents "to fill the bucket of their child's self-esteem so high that the world will not be able to poke enough holes in it to drain it dry."[2] A father who does this deserves the highest honor—and the most respect—of any man on earth.

Even God the Father, in the face of so many possibilities for a title by which we could address Him—simply chose Father. How wise we would all be to recognize—and then let our actions show—that this is, without a doubt, the title most noble of all.

1. Harold B. Lee, "Strengthening the Home," pamphlet (Salt Lake City: The Church of Jesus Christ of Latter-day Saints, 1973), 7.
2. Alvin Price, in Thomas E. Kelley, *Father's Gifts* (Salt Lake City: Deseret Book Company, 1984), 8.

· FORGIVENESS ·

Freedom through Forgiveness

ALL THE GREAT FAITHS OF THE WORLD teach the power of forgiveness. In the Sermon on the Mount, Jesus explains the principle with unmistakable clarity: "For if ye forgive men their trespasses, your heavenly Father will also forgive you: But if ye forgive not men their trespasses, neither will your Father forgive your trespasses."[1]

Unfortunately, many of us find it exceedingly difficult to forgive others. We speak of forgiveness with our lips but hoard stale bitterness in our hearts. Two insights may help free us of this toxic burden.

First, we need to remember the wisdom of an old folk saying: "A grudge rots the pocket it is kept in." A young teacher interviewed a school principal retiring after years of service. The principal had dealt with many conflicts during her administration, including curriculum quarrels, staffing disagreements, and even racial tensions. Despite excellent leadership, she had been the target of harsh words and deeds from many directions, yet she harbored no resentment toward any person or group. The young teacher expressed admiration for the principal's great kindness in this respect. The older woman smiled and said, "Yes, by forgiving I have been kind, it is true—kind to *myself* more than to anyone

64

else." A grudge that is harbored becomes an infection festering within us. By obeying the commandment to forgive, we protect our own spiritual health.

We can also become more skilled at forgiving if we bear in mind what is required of us. To forgive does not mean saying that a hurtful deed was "all right" or that it "didn't matter." It means releasing our desire for retribution, for hurting those who have hurt us. Dr. Carolyn Myss writes: "The true nature of forgiveness remains misunderstood. . . . Forgiveness is [an act] that liberates . . . the soul from the need for personal vengeance."[2]

We need never condone wrongdoing. But we can wisely recognize that judgment belongs to God and that we are called to live and to love in the present. We cannot feed our souls today with yesterday's leftovers. True forgiveness leaves the past behind. Each time an old offense comes to mind, we can simply say, "That chapter is closed." We can bring our focus back to the opportunities and the duties of the present moment. Untended, the fires of anger and resentment will eventually die out. At that point we are liberated from the infection of the past. Then, as Paul promised the Colossians, we become a new and stronger people, "Forbearing one another, and forgiving one another."[3]

1. *New Testament*, Matthew 6:14–15.
2. Carolyn Myss, *Anatomy of the Spirit* (New York City: Crown Publishers, 1996), 235–36.
3. *New Testament*, Colossians 3:13.

"And If Thou Wilt, Forget"

IN ONE OF HER POEMS, the well-known Victorian writer Christina Rossetti makes known her wishes in the event of her death. Do not, she implores, sing sad songs or plant the traditional cypress tree or rose bush in her memory. Instead, Rossetti begs, simply do two things:

> And if thou wilt, remember,
> And if thou wilt, forget.[1]

With these haunting lyrics, Rossetti touches on a universal human desire—that the special people in our lives might somehow remember our strengths while overlooking our faults, our moments of ill temper, pettiness, or unkindness. If we could, we might speak the poet's words to them ourselves: "And if thou wilt, forget."

One woman recalls an important lesson she learned about forgetting. Tired, worried, and temporarily overwhelmed by the responsibility of caring for an elderly parent, this woman lost her temper with her brother. In a fit of anger, she accused him of neglecting their mother, of not fulfilling his family obligations, of leaving her with all the work. In reality, none of this was true; and, when her anger subsided, as anger always does, this good woman was appalled by her own unfairness. When she called her brother the next morning to apologize, she found herself unexpectedly moved by his response. "Not to worry," he said. "All is forgotten."

We may not always be fortunate enough to deal with people who are willing to forget our shortcomings, but we ourselves can make the decision to practice the fine art of compassionate forgetting. We can choose to forget the unintentionally thoughtless remark made by a coworker. We can choose to forget the irritable outburst of a loving spouse. We can choose to forget the fury directed at us by a frustrated child. We can choose to take the poet's words to heart: "And if thou wilt, forget."

Forgetting in this manner is really an act of forgiveness—the same kind of forgiveness we desire when, fully aware of our own imperfections, we approach a loving God and cry with the words of today's choir selection, "Lord, have mercy."[2]

May we be as merciful in our memories of others as our divine Creator is with us.

1. Christina Rossetti, "A Song," in *Victorian Poetry and Poetics* (Boston: Houghton Mifflin Company, 1968), 601.
2. S. V. Lvovsky, "Hospodi Pomilui" ("Lord, Have Mercy on Us"), revised and adapted with English text added by Louis Koppitz (Boston: E. C. Shirmer Music Company, 1948).

Forgiving Yourself

IN A CANDID MOMENT BORN OF FATIGUE, a loving, conscientious mother of five lively children confessed to her teenage son that she had always found it very difficult to admit her mistakes. She knew she was slow to acknowledge when she was at fault—slow to offer an apology to the family and friends she adored.

The wisdom of the boy's response surprised her: "Maybe you have a hard time forgiving yourself," he said.

This young man correctly perceived that the pain of making mistakes may cause us to avoid confronting our errors. It is as though we feel we cannot possibly be worthwhile if we are less than perfect. And yet, as the Greek dramatist Euripides noted: "Men are men, they needs must err."[1] To be human, almost by definition, means that we will sometimes stumble.

How wonderful is the practice of self-forgiveness then! Self-forgiveness is the assurance that we are still valuable in spite of our errors. Self-forgiveness is permission to get up, dust ourselves off, and try it again. Self-forgiveness is the psychological equivalent of a second chance.

The benefits of forgiving ourselves are many. When we forgive ourselves for our own shortcomings, we actually take an important step toward overcoming them. We can acknowledge

our faults and move to correct them instead of becoming paralyzed by a sense of our inadequacy.

When we forgive ourselves for our own weaknesses, we greet
the people in our lives with tolerant hearts. Responding to our
friends and family members with an attitude of acceptance, rather
than accusation, creates a climate of trust and warmth in which
relationships can flourish.

And finally, when we freely forgive ourselves and others, we
invite a spirit of peace to reside with us—the kind of divine peace
celebrated in song: "There'll be love and forgiveness, there'll be
peace and contentment, there'll be joy, joy, joy . . ."[2]

1. Euripides, in *The Harper Book of Quotations,* 3rd edition, ed. Robert I. Fitzhenry (New
  York City: HarperPerennial, 1993), 302.
2. Natalie Sleeth, "Joy in the Morning" (n.p.: Hope Publishing Company, n.d.).

"The Quality of Mercy"

ALL TOO OFTEN, WE LIMIT our consideration of the concept of
mercy to matters of law. In courts across our countries, we may
plead for leniency—either for ourselves or for the accused—when
the demands of justice seem too high, hoping that those who render verdicts will temper their rulings with an appropriate degree
of compassion. And as we anticipate making an accounting of our
lives when we leave this mortal sphere, we want to trust in God's
promise of never-ending mercy.

Mercy, though, need not be reserved for the stately halls of
justice or the judgment bar of God; rather, it can influence all of
our interactions with others. Yet, in our day-to-day lives our incli-
nations are sometimes reminiscent of the words of the British
writer George Eliot, who said: "We hand folks over to God's
mercy, and show none ourselves."[1]

We forget, as we deal harshly with those we feel have wronged us—whether they be husbands or wives, sons or daughters, neighbors or strangers—that

> The quality of mercy is not strain'd,
> It droppeth as the gentle rain from heaven
> Upon the place beneath: it is twice bless'd;
> It blesseth him that gives and him that takes.[2]

Instead, our natural tendency when we feel we've been wronged is to lash out, to seek for vengeance, to require repayment, or to find some other way to make things right for us. We forget the good that comes from forgiveness—and the soothing effect such an act can have on both the person forgiven and the person forgiving.

As we face the affronts that are part of the inevitability of life, we ought to remember the attributes that Nehemiah of old ascribed to God. Wrote the prophet, "Thou art a God ready to pardon, gracious and merciful, slow to anger, and of great kindness."[3]

Certainly, there are situations when justice must be meted out in full measure, when those who have wronged must be corrected with firmness if they are to learn. But there are perhaps many more times when a moment's pause would suggest that we show forbearance, forgiveness, and concern. For, when our actions toward others are patterned after the attributes of God, we are, indeed, "twice blessed."

1. George Eliot, *Adam Bede* (New York City: Airmont Publishing, 1966), 332.
2. William Shakespeare, *The Merchant of Venice*, act IV, scene 1, lines 184–87, *The Complete Works of William Shakespeare* (London: Spring Books, 1958).
3. *Old Testament*, Nehemiah 9:17.

Forgiveness

"Slow to Anger"

INDIVIDUALS WHO DELIBERATELY decide not to take offense lead happier, more productive lives.

It is probably safe to say that we have all been offended at one time or another. Our daily involvement with other people—family, friends, acquaintances, neighbors, coworkers, and even the strangers we pass on the streets—practically guarantees that opportunities for receiving offense will arise. And when we are offended, we respond by feeling confused, hurt, even angry. Sometimes we may become aggressively hostile in return: words are spoken and relationships are strained. Witness the feuds that have erupted into deadly conflicts among friends, neighbors, and even nations because someone, somewhere, took offense.

It is important to remember that, in most cases, offense was never intended in the first place. The people in our lives may say or do things that are hurtful out of carelessness or a lack of knowledge rather than out of malice or spite. We ourselves have all been guilty of this same kind of thoughtlessness. That is why it makes sense to heed the advice found in Proverbs to be "slow to anger."[1]

When we choose not to take offense, we actually free ourselves to become happier individuals. Certainly, we are happier in our relationships. When we approach the associates who have offended us with calm kindness instead of hostility, focusing on their strengths and triumphs instead of on their weaknesses and failures, we ultimately engender goodwill on both sides. Instead of tallying up slights and nursing grievances, we reach out with both hands and enjoy the short time we have here on earth with one another.

When we refuse to take offense, we also free ourselves to become more productive in our personal and professional lives. Anger clouds the head, making it difficult to concentrate on our various tasks. It also interferes with our ability to make clear, insightful decisions.

How much better it is, then, to actively sideline our resentment and invite peace to rule in our minds and hearts.

1. *Old Testament,* Proverbs 16:32.

· FRIENDSHIP ·

Souls Knit Together

O[UR LIVES WOULD BE LONELY] and empty, indeed, were we to travel through this world without the love and the support of friends.

"Next to kinship with God," said David O. McKay, "comes the helpfulness, encouragement, and inspiration of friends. Friendship is a sacred possession." He continued, "As air, water, and sunshine [are] to flowers, . . . so smiles, sympathy, and love [are] to the daily life of man."[1]

Surely, we recognize the richness that is added to our lives when we enjoy meaningful friendships—when we feel for others and express those feelings in thoughtful ways and when we are touched by the gentle concern of those with whom we share this great gift.

Yet, many of us are also aware, whether through observation or our own experiences, that in these modern times true friendships are sometimes woefully lacking. In our neighborhoods we sometimes are much more concerned about isolating and protecting ourselves than about giving of ourselves to those with whom we share a common community. In the workplace we often are overwhelmed by the pressures to perform, and so we worry needlessly about others getting ahead of us in a race that really has no end. And in other settings we settle for the superficial rather than striving to plant and care for the seeds that can grow into rich and rewarding relationships.

We ought to find ways in the midst of our busy days to cultivate friendships with those around us—not for some strategic advantage, but for the simple reason that we need to be connected to those with whom we live.

We ought to be willing to make commitments to others—commitments that lead us to lift the heavy arms of one who has been worn down by the worries of the world, to share with another the joy we've felt after a particularly fulfilling day, to do for others those things that they cannot do for themselves.

And we ought to be more concerned, day to day, with taking care of our friendships than with some of the other, less important things that tend to top our "to-do" lists.

In the Old Testament we read that "the soul of Jonathan was knit with the soul of David, and Jonathan loved him as his own soul."[2]

In our own times our souls will surely be filled as we learn to become better friends, for friendship, in the words of one who knew, "unites the human family with its happy influence."[3]

1. David O. McKay, *Gospel Ideals* (Salt Lake City: *The Improvement Era,* 1953), 253.

2. *Old Testament,* 1 Samuel 18:1.

3. Joseph Smith, *The Teachings of the Prophet Joseph Smith,* comp. Joseph Fielding Smith (Salt Lake City: Deseret Book Company, 1970), 316.

A Checklist for Friendship

GOOD FRIENDS ARE A BLESSING. Their presence at life's wide table enhances all our experience, sharpening the joy we feel at happy moments while tempering our pain during times of sorrow. We may well agree with Aristotle when he said that "without friends, no one would choose to live, though he had all other goods."[1]

Most of us would also agree with that great philosopher when he remarked, "We should behave to our friends as we would wish our friends to behave to us."[2] This observation is so fundamental, so obvious, that the expression of it almost seems trite. Naturally, it only makes sense to treat our friends with the consideration and affection we ourselves desire. And yet, it is surprising how often we neglect to follow Aristotle's basic advice.

A woman with a special talent for cultivating friendships recalls the uncomfortable surprise she felt when she realized that she, of all people, had slipped into a pattern of benign neglect where her many friends were concerned. She had become so busy with family and work responsibilities that she no longer did the things she used to do routinely: remember birthdays with a call, invite people over for an informal bowl of ice cream on Sunday evenings, pick a quick bouquet of flowers from her garden to send along with a note. None of these gestures was elaborate, yet each had been genuinely appreciated by her friends.

Ultimately, this woman decided to take the venerable Samuel Johnson's admonition to heart: "A man, Sir, should keep his friendship in constant repair."[3] She made a list of the qualities a good friend should have, then periodically checked herself against it in the quiet of the early morning hours before the noise of her day began.

Each of us may wish to develop our own checklist—formal or informal—with the intent of keeping, in the words of Johnson, "our friendship in constant repair." We can ask ourselves pertinent questions: Am I patient? Am I considerate? Am I courteous? Do I forgive? Do I really listen to the answers my friends give when I ask them questions? Can I compromise? Do I know when to say something—and when to remain quiet? Am I discreet? Do I know when it is in the best interest of my friends to mind my own business? Do I celebrate the qualities that make my friends uniquely themselves?

In the end, this kind of regular attention to friendship is nothing less than a standing invitation to the people we care about to join us and share life's many and varied adventures.

---

1. Aristotle, in *The Harper Book of Quotations*, 3rd edition, ed. Robert I. Fitzhenry (New York City: HarperPerennial, 1993), 166.
2. Samuel Johnson, in *Bartlett's Familiar Quotations*, 15th edition, ed. John Bartlett (Boston: Little, Brown and Company, 1980), 87.
3. Ibid., 354.

Good Neighbors

IN HIS POEM "MENDING WALL," Robert Frost writes of an annual spring ritual in which he and his neighbor mend the wall that divides their properties. The neighbor, stubbornly insisting that "good fences make good neighbors," walks the wall line with the poet, noting areas of disrepair, while Frost laments: "He is all pine, and I am apple orchard. I tell him my apple trees will never get across and eat the cones under his pines. He only says, 'Good fences make good neighbors.'" But, says Frost, "Something there is that doesn't love a wall."[1]

Much of civilization depends, it is true, on proper boundaries, borders, and distinctions between peoples, communities, neighbors. However, in a world grown increasingly fearful and reclusive, the need to break through such barriers has become, paradoxically, nearly as important as the barriers themselves. We need human connection, it seems, as much as we need privacy. For far too many of us, the locked and bolted front door has replaced the communal front porch, and television has replaced evenings that might otherwise have been filled with conversation.

While good fences can make for good neighbors, all good fences need gates.

As Neil Postman has pointed out, the phrase "reach out and touch someone" has come to mean a brief conversation by telephone with a distant relative. "The 'someone' used to play a daily and vital role in our lives; used to be a member of the family." Laments Postman, sometimes it seems "American culture stands vigorously opposed to the idea of family."[2]

"Something there is that doesn't love a wall." Despite the frantic pace of life and the genuine fears that can so easily consume us, there is still room in the world for the simple joys of neighborliness. A plate of warm cookies, a shared chore, or a friendly chat can break down a wall as surely as the spring thaw.

In a world grown chilly, we need the warmth of a handclasp or greeting. Surely our yards need fences; our properties need walls. But, just as surely, homes need good neighbors. And all of us, always, need the closeness of true friends.

---

1. Robert Frost, *Robert Frost's Poems* (New York City: Washington Square Press, 1971), 94.
2. Neil Postman, *Amusing Ourselves to Death* (New York City: Viking Penguin, 1985), 134.

· GRATITUDE ·

Gratitude—Thanks in Deed

CONVALESCING AFTER A LONG and serious illness, Grace Noll Crowell penned the words of the beautiful hymn "Because I Have Been Given Much." According to Crowell, the hymn was written "in a sudden, glad up-rush of gratitude for my release from pain, recalling the many mercies that had been mine those long, hard days, and . . . remembering the love that had been around and about me ever."[1]

Hymns like "Because I Have Been Given Much" remind us that our gratitude to God and others is best expressed not by what we say, but by how we live. As such hymns suggest, our expressions of thanks and praise to those who have blessed our lives are the beginning, not the end, of true gratitude.

Through recognizing the generosity of others and the goodness of God, it becomes easier for us to be generous and good ourselves. From the roots of simple gratitude grow a multitude of crowning virtues, including mercy, benevolence, and love. As we express our gratitude, not only in word but also in deed, we quickly discover that our happiness and contentment depend much less on our material possessions and much more on how well we recognize and appreciate all that we have.

True gratitude is the beginning of greatness, because it stems from our acknowledging our dependence on deity in a way that links us to our fellowman. Such gratitude is a daily lifestyle, not a passing emotion. The true measure of our gratitude is how we live after we have offered a thankful prayer, penned a sincere thank you note, or acknowledged the thoughtful act of another.

As Joseph F. Smith wrote, "The spirit of gratitude is always pleasant and satisfying because it carries with it a sense of helpfulness to others; it begets love and friendship, and engenders divine influence. Gratitude is said to be the memory of the heart."[2]

When our hearts are filled with grateful memories, our actions reflect the love that we have received and we begin to express our gratitude to God as described in the last verse of Crowell's hymn: "Because I have been blessed by thy great love, dear Lord, I'll share thy love again, according to thy word. I shall give love to those in need; I'll show that love by word and deed. Thus shall my thanks be thanks indeed."[3]

---

1. John Barnes Pratt, *Present Day Hymns and How They Were Written* (New York City: A. S. Barnes and Company, 1940), 27, as quoted in Karen Lynn Davidson, *Our Latter-day Hymns: The Stories and the Messages* (Salt Lake City: Deseret Book Company, 1988), 230–31.
2. Joseph F. Smith, *Gospel Doctrine* (Salt Lake City: Deseret Book Company, 1963), 262.
3. "Because I Have Been Given Much," text by Grace Noll Crowell and music by Phillip Landgrave, *Hymns of The Church of Jesus Christ of Latter-day Saints* (Salt Lake City: The Church of Jesus Christ of Latter-day Saints, 1985), no. 219.

The Riches of Gratitude

T RULY RICH IS THE PERSON with a grateful heart. Grateful individuals possess a treasure that cannot be stolen or spent, because it comes from character and perspective, not circumstances. The riches of gratitude can be ours whenever we are willing to acknowledge the goodness of God and the many ways that other lives influence and bless our own.

What a powerful quality gratitude is! It's been said that "we have all drunk from wells we have not dug and warmed ourselves by fires we have not kindled."[1] Yet, too frequently we fail to recognize the multitude of well diggers and fire builders around us. Our ability to appreciate the roles that family, friends, and others play in our lives both enriches us and blesses those for whom we are grateful.

Gratitude also means recognizing all that God has given us. The wealth of a grateful heart is not diminished by daily downturns or even life's tragedies, secure in the knowledge that God lives and that He loves His children. When our hearts are filled with gratitude, our moments of mourning, fear, and despair are swallowed up in the overwhelming manifestations of God's love for us.

True gratitude stems from a personal relationship with deity; never from comparing ourselves with others. Grateful people are happy, not because they have more than others, but because they see the hand of God in their own lives and remember the great things He has done for them. How sweet is the sleep of one who kneels each night to thank God for each blessing of that day. How rich is the person who awakens each morning with gratitude for another day of life.

Our lives forever change when we attune our hearts to hear "the still small voice of gratitude."[2] Listening to gratitude's gentle whisperings, it is much easier for us to worship God, to love and serve our fellow men, and to live in thanksgiving daily.[3]

Worldly wealth is fleeting; material possessions can be lost or worn out. But those who have a grateful heart possess a treasure they will share throughout their lives and find laid up for them in heaven.

---

1. Richard L. Simpson, *The Replenishment Principle at BYU*, compiled for the BYU Alumni Past Presidents' Council by David P. Forsyth, 11 October 1996, 1.

2. John Bartlett, ed., *Bartlett's Familiar Quotations*, 15th edition (Boston: Little, Brown and Company, 1980), 363.

3. *Book of Mormon*, Alma 34:28.

Praise His Holy Name

W HEN EVERYTHING IN LIFE IS GOING WELL, it's easy to praise God. Some days our gardens bloom, our bills are paid, our children are full of affectionate hugs, and our neighbors are extra cordial. It's easy, then, to sing, like David of old, "I give thanks unto thee, O Lord, and sing praises unto thy name."[1]

But all days are not sunny ones, bills pile up, and all children have moments of ingratitude. And yet, it's just when things are at their most difficult—the times when we feel least blessed—that we most need to bless His holy name.

Job understood this principle. At the height of personal tragedy, a moment when all his life's fondest hopes and possessions lay in ruin, he kneeled before his God and prayed, "The Lord gave, and the Lord hath taken away; blessed be the name of the Lord."[2]

As a family gathered around the hospital bed of a beloved grandmother, a young grandson was asked to offer a family prayer. At first, he thought to refuse, thinking of the pain suffered by someone he loved and how much it hurt to watch her endure it. But as he opened his heart to his Father in Heaven, to his surprise the words that came out of his mouth were words of thanksgiving and praise. With a heart full of gratitude, he found himself thanking God for letting him be a part of his grandmother's life. He thanked God for her great spirit and for the love the whole family had shared. And he knew a greater peace than he had ever felt. And he knew, looking at his grandmother, that she felt the same peace.

When we brood and worry about what's wrong with our lives, fear and pain can begin to define who we are. But when we focus on the great blessings in our lives, then God's richness and love become a part of our souls. We can become more like Him whom we praise; let us all sing our praises to God.

1. *Old Testament,* Psalm 18:49.

2. *Old Testament,* Job 1:21.

A Prayer of Thanksgiving

In a world where our wants seem to know no bounds, where our lists of desires seem to stretch on forever, we might do well at times to take this simpler view: "It is not the things we have that makes us happy. It is the things we feel."[1]

And there is no more ennobling feeling than that of gratitude—the sense that we have, indeed, been given much. When we dwell too much upon all the things we think we need, we find ourselves weighted down by worries over which we have little control; but when our hearts are filled with thoughts of thanksgiving, we can find relief from our burdens and uncover greater meaning and richness in life.

A day of thanksgiving is an important part of many cultures. It is a custom we should always take time to observe as we turn our attention toward the bounties we enjoy; but this one day each year could then be followed by 364 others that find us regularly reflecting upon the innumerable blessings we have been given.

The poet Samuel Johnson wrote, "Gratitude is a fruit of great cultivation."[2] And the Psalmist set forth an important part of the process of cultivating a grateful heart when he declared, "Let us come before [God's] presence with thanksgiving."[3]

Sometimes, though, our prayers can take the form of perpetual petitions as we offer brief and sweeping expressions of gratitude to the giver of all good things—and then turn immediately to all that we hope to obtain at His hand. What effect might it have on our hearts if, even occasionally, we offered up our grateful hearts to God, expressing only appreciation for all that we have—and asking nothing in return?

We might remember the blessings of children who have grown to be our friends, good health long taken for granted, shelter from winter's winds, friends who still think to call, a meal that once kept us from hunger. We might pause to recall a song that brought back a fond memory, a talent we've been able to share, a kindness extended us by a stranger. We might gaze in our mind's eye at a sunrise that overcame a dark night, at the stars that connect us to heaven, at mountains from which we derive strength. We might ponder a lesson learned, a promise kept, a hope renewed.

There is no limit to the thanks we can offer up to heaven when we approach prayer with a grateful heart. And there is no end to the good that comes as we dwell less upon all that we think we need and more upon all that we have.

1. George Albert Smith, *Sharing the Gospel with Others* (Salt Lake City: Deseret News Press, 1948), 108.
2. Samuel Johnson, *Tour to the Hebrides* (Oxford, England: Oxford University Press, 1924), 315.
3. *Old Testament,* Psalm 95:2.

· HOPE ·

"Hope Springs Exulting"

HOPE IS A UNIVERSAL YEARNING that makes possible the lives we live. We have hope that, when we awake in the morning, the sun will arise as well. We sow seeds, convinced that crops will one day spring forth. We marry and bring children into the world, believing we will find happiness as we create a home.

In the words of the poet Robert Burns, "Hope springs exulting on triumphant wing."[1]

Or, as expressed by another, "A person without hope is like a person without a heart; there is nothing to keep him going."[2]

What we hope for, however, should be shaped by those values that transcend the world's standards of success. We may wish for riches, for fame, or for glamour, but then be disappointed when we fail to realize what may have been rather unrealistic ambitions. Conversely, we may hope for peace within our homes, for the strength to deal honestly with others, or for the ability to have a positive influence in our community, and then be pleasantly surprised by the effects of our ongoing efforts.

Of course, we will all experience difficulties that challenge even the most optimistic among us; and when we are being buffeted by one of life's storms, we may find it difficult to see the proverbial silver lining of the clouds that engulf us.

Depression and despair can, indeed, be overwhelming, particularly when we are faced with adversity or tragedy; but by carefully cultivating our faith and hope, we will be better able to withstand whatever we may encounter.

One young mother, when told by her doctors that she was terminally ill, refused to give up and resolved to continue to find ways to serve others—as she had for so many years before. Although the end ultimately came, a loving husband said this about the underlying hope that sustained her: "I watched service consume pain. I witnessed faith destroy discouragement. I [saw] courage magnify her beyond her natural abilities."[3]

Though our circumstances differ greatly, there are so many sources of hope: the wonders of the world around us, the reciprocal love of family and friends, the teachings of wise men and women. And as we cultivate the kind of hope that abides, we will have the joy that endures.

---

1. Robert Burns, "The Cotter's Saturday Night," line 138, in *English Romantic Poetry and Prose,* ed. Russell Noyes (New York City: Oxford University Press, 1956), 155.
2. John H. Groberg, "There Is Always Hope," in *1983–84 Fireside and Devotional Speeches* (Provo, Utah: Brigham Young University Publications, 1984), 136.
3. L. Tom Perry, "A Tribute," *Ensign,* May 1975, 33.

The Hope for a Better World

TODAY'S WORLD SURROUNDS US with many negative images—crime and violence, cruelty and poverty—but as long as we refuse to give up hope, a better world will come. During life's struggles and trials, our hope for a better world can give us the courage to act and the strength to endure. For if we believe that our lives and the world can be made better, that hope will dispel feelings of helplessness and despair and fill our daily activities with vitality and direction.

When viewed with hope, the world opens endless possibilities for us to change and grow and learn—if only we believe it possible. Consider the lesson learned by a loving grandmother, who watched the full moon rise with her three-year-old granddaughter on a family camping trip. The little girl noticed that, with each step she took closer to a nearby tree, part of the moon would disappear from view, obscured by the tree's trunk and branches. Filled with wonder, the three-year-old turned and said, "Look, Grandma, I can move the moon!"

Likewise, our small, but hopeful, steps can change our perspective. The world is ours to move and to mold if we believe in a better tomorrow—and work towards it today. Hoping and dreaming of a better world are not enough if we are unwilling to work; but when we work towards our dreams, wonderful things can happen.

Even our most tedious and routine daily tasks become easier and more meaningful if we see them as helping to make the world a better place. By changing a diaper, washing the dishes, or mowing a neighbor's lawn, we are making the world better for someone. And although we may not always love what life requires us to do, we can always love why we do it.

Henry David Thoreau wrote, "If one advances confidently in the direction of his dreams, and endeavors to live the life which he has imagined, he will meet with success unexpected in common hours."[1] And so it is with us. We can be men and women who hope and dream that our lives, our families, and the world can be better than they are while we work to make it so.

As we do, we will see that our present problems are not invincible, nor are the world's ills incurable. For every morning comes to each of us wrapped in the hope that the world can and will be a better place for having lived that day. And while the world may not be perfect tomorrow, if we continue to allow our hopes and dreams to vitalize our work—someday, somehow, some-way—it will be.

1. Henry David Thoreau, *Walden* (New York City: Macmillian Publishing Company, 1961), 228.

· J U D G I N G ·

Looking on the Heart

LONG AGO, THE PROPHET SAMUEL was taught: "The Lord seeth not as man seeth; for man looketh on the outward appearance, but the Lord looketh on the heart."[1] This passage of scripture is familiar to many. But, like Samuel, we may find it difficult at times not to be distracted—or even misled—by appearances.

Samuel was struggling to find a replacement for King Saul when the Lord gave him this counsel: "Look not on [the] countenance, or on the height of his stature," but rather look on the heart.[2] He was still mourning the downfall of this great leader when, as prophet, he was commanded to anoint a new king. At that point in time, looking on the heart of any other man—even a future king—required the opening of his own heart.

And so it goes for each of us. Think how our lives are enriched when we choose to look on the heart—and when others look on ours. How we value the friend who at first seemed so different from us, but whom we took the time to get to know. How we cherish the family member who sees past our shortcomings and never fails to find goodness in us. For who we are on the inside—how we think and feel—matters so much more than what we appear to be.

Appearances can be deceptive, to be sure. The clothing we

87

wear, the company we keep, the car we drive, the house we occupy are all outward measurements that can keep us from each other's hearts. They allow for quick and easy classifications. But the stature of a person's soul is so much more difficult to qualify, let alone discern.

Henry David Thoreau had much to say about looking deeper: "We know but few men," he wrote, and "a great many coats and breeches." But, as Thoreau decides, "If my jacket and trousers, my hat and shoes, are fit to worship God in, they will do, will they not?"[3]

Certainly, the Lord is less concerned about outward appearances. His all-seeing eye penetrates to the very heart and discovers there the greatest treasure. He sees goodness, because He is good. He knows truth, because He is truth. He discerns real love, because He is love.

The more our own hearts are full of His goodness, truth, and love, the more we will be able to see as the Lord sees and really look on the heart.

---

1. *Old Testament,* 1 Samuel 16:7.
2. Ibid.
3. Henry David Thoreau, *Walden and Civil Disobedience* (New York City: Penguin Classics, 1983), 66.

"With What Judgment Ye Judge"

COMMON TO VIRTUALLY ALL RELIGIONS is the concept of a day of judgment—that moment when each of us will be required to give an accounting of how we have lived our lives and those things we have chosen to do or not do. While anticipating such a time may cause understandable concern, we find comfort in knowing that

He who will judge possesses knowledge, wisdom, and a sense of mercy that transcends our limited understanding.

Our own mortal views of one another's actions are not nearly as clear, however. Often we are all too willing to interpret motives, to criticize the decisions of those we know, to condemn actions we deem unacceptable. In our own minds and in more public forums, we call others before the bar of judgment, we act as judge and jury, and we render our verdicts after hearing only our side of the case. Then we mete out punishment of alienation, of public criticism, and even retribution.

Rather than concerning ourselves with our own shortcomings, we cast a watchful eye upon the actions of others, often arriving at conclusions we later find were unwarranted. Such was the case in one of our cities when several leading citizens began to notice unexplained changes in a man well known to them. Whereas he had once taken an active part in many community events, he started to stay away from such activities and then became somewhat distant and distracted. Soon his friends began suggesting to one another that something must have soured him on his previous involvements and that his actions likely stemmed from his being a poor sport or perceiving offenses where there had been none. Before long, his associates avoided him whenever they could and sought to exclude him from their circles.

As so often happens, when this man was later diagnosed with a brain tumor that explained the changes in his behavior, his friends felt ashamed of their combined rush to judgment.[1]

When the Old Testament prophet Samuel was charged with selecting a successor to King Saul, he was initially distracted by issues that were of no interest to the God of Israel. Finally, Samuel was instructed: "Look not on his countenance, or on the height of his stature; because I . . . the Lord seeth not as man seeth; for man looketh on the outward appearance, but the Lord looketh on the heart."[2]

Before we arrive at conclusions concerning another's actions, before we pass along tales of another's misdeeds, before we spend our time probing for vices rather than virtues, we would do well to recognize our own lack of omniscient insight and to remember that "with what judgment [we] judge, [we] shall be judged."[3]

1. N. Eldon Tanner, *Seek Ye First the Kingdom of God* (Salt Lake City: Deseret Book Company, 1973), 54.
2. *Old Testament*, 1 Samuel 16:7.
3. *New Testament*, Matthew 7:2.

Seeking Sound Judgment

A CRITIC OF MODERN CULTURE once asked, "Why do so many people pray to acquire good fortune, and so few pray to acquire good judgment?"[1]

Why, indeed, do we turn our heads so readily toward the illusions of wealth and the mirages of pride and pretense, when what will ultimately benefit us most is greater insight, discernment, wisdom, and judgment?

In some form or another—to some degree or another—we exercise our judgment almost every minute of every day. We decide, with or without much thought, what to wear in the morning, what we'll give our attention to at work, how we'll spend our free time. We determine, consciously or otherwise, how we will treat a spouse, how we will interact with a friend, how we will deal with a difficult child. We choose how to face an unexpected challenge, how best to settle a dispute, how to resolve a crisis of faith.

And, to greater or lesser degrees, we can see the effects of poor judgment without having to look very far. Fortunes are lost through bad judgment. Children are alienated through careless interactions. Marriages are destroyed through careless decisions.

To avoid the consequences of such ill-advised actions, we

may wish to spend some time each day feeding our minds and our souls with worthwhile instruction—whether it comes from the books we read, the media we allow to influence us, or the moments we take for quiet reflection. We may, when needed, ask for the counsel of a wise parent, a trusted associate, a counselor, or a religious leader. And we can seek out spiritual sources that will support us when significant decisions are faced.

Given the elusive nature of the riches we so often seek to acquire, we would do well to seek instead for sound insight and judgment. Then, in the words of Neal A. Maxwell, we will be better able to make judgments based on "the things that matter most, so that those things are not at the mercy of the things that matter least."[2]

---

1. Sidney J. Harris, *Clearing the Ground* (Boston: Houghton Mifflin, 1986), 73.
2. Neal A. Maxwell, *Deposition of a Disciple* (Salt Lake City: Deseret Book Company, 1976), 58.

· LIFE ·

Living and Growing

OF ALL THE BOUNTIES THAT LIFE offers us, our daily opportunities for personal growth are among the most unappreciated. Each new day can bring learning and progress, but only if we are willing to grow. In the words of Cardinal Newman, "Growth is the only evidence of life."[1]

Much as a flower blooms, becoming more beautiful day by day, so we too may become a little better each day of our lives. A rosebud becomes a rose simply by daily opening itself to take in a little more of the sunlight. And so it is with us.

Our ability to continue to learn and grow throughout our lives is more a matter of attitude than age. Each day we can be more happy, more faithful, more compassionate, and more patient—for life's short growing season is much too brief to be squandered.

Our lives will not blossom overnight; but one petal at a time, we can grow in the light that comes from God, our loving Creator, whose plan for us to become like Him requires incremental, sometimes almost imperceptible progress. The scriptures teach that we become partakers of the divine nature by taking one step at a time, diligently adding one virtue to another.[2]

A lifetime of growth awaits if we simply live each day to the fullest and avoid stagnation. Leonardo da Vinci warned, "Iron rusts from disuse, stagnant water loses its purity . . . ; even so does inaction sap the vigor of the mind."[3] Our willingness to act, to adapt, to overcome, and to grow measures not only who we are, but also what we become.

As long as we are living, we can continue learning and growing, but only if we keep trying. Each day we can look for chances to stretch our souls, realizing that life often disguises opportunities for growth as trials, disappointments, and even monotony.

God is the perfect gardener. He will provide each of His children with the right combination of pruning, sunlight, and rain to help us blossom.

1. Cardinal Newman, in *Bartlett's Familiar Quotations*, 15th edition, ed. John Bartlett (Boston: Little, Brown and Company, 1980), 361.
2. *New Testament*, 2 Peter 1:5–7.
3. Leonardo da Vinci, *The Notebooks of Leonardo da Vinci*, ed. Edward MacCurdy (New York City: Reynal & Hitchcock, 1938), 1:96.

Bad Days and Rays of Sunshine

IN THIS WORLD, FULL OF STUBBED TOES and traffic jams, it's easy to give feelings of irritability and frustration too much space in our lives. A missed appointment, an ache or a pain, a brief moment of rudeness can color our mood for hours. Like Alexander, the young boy in Judith Viorst's children's classic *Alexander and the Terrible, Horrible, No Good, Very Bad Day,* we can easily come to feel that a day in which we had beans for dinner and no dessert for lunch and in which the dentist finds a cavity is a day irreparably ruined.[1]

Bad days and minor irritations are a part of our existence here on earth. But God, in His infinite wisdom, has given us an earth that compensates downpours with rainbows and potholes with grand canyons. As scientist Stephen Jay Gould has written: "Many things keep us going in this vale of tears—a baby's smile, Bach's B-minor Mass, a decent bagel. Every once in a while, as if to grant us the courage to go on, the powers that be turn one of life's little disasters into a bit of joy or an episode of instruction."[2] Or as Robert Frost puts it:

> The way a crow
> Shook down on me
> The dust of snow
> From a hemlock tree
> Has given my heart
> A change of mood
> And saved some part
> Of a day I had rued.[3]

In a world such as this one, we will inevitably run across our measure of aggravations and annoyances. But if we are careful to look for them, we will find compensations as well—rare moments of unexpected beauty or unforeseen pleasure: a good meal, a glorious sunset, a smile, the sudden warmth of a new friendship, or an unforeseen compliment from an unanticipated source.

Amidst the vexing, exasperating trials of everyday life, let us remember that God has not abandoned us and that His works always leave behind a trace of His presence. Let us learn to overlook the irritations of the world and bask, instead, in the richness life can offer.

1. Judith Viorst, *Alexander and the Terrible, Horrible, No Good, Very Bad Day* (Hartford: Connecticut Printers, 1972).
2. Stephen Jay Gould, *Dinosaur in a Haystack: Reflections on Natural History* (New York City: Harmony Book, 1995), 5.
3. Robert Frost, "Dust of Snow," *Robert Frost's Poems,* ed. Louis Untermeyer (New York City: Washington Square Press, 1946), 240.

Broadening Our Perspectives

As a lone hiker began the long ascent to the top of a nearby mountain, he noticed that, each time he looked down from the trail, his eyes immediately returned to a parking lot near where he had started his trek. For well over an hour he climbed, yet he kept seeing the same view every time he turned around.

Eventually, his eyes began to see more broadly. First he saw the tip of a distant, prominent peak that had been blocked from his view. Then he saw the edge of a nearby lake; after he had climbed farther, he saw the lake in its entirety. After another hour on the trail, he saw a small hamlet some 40 miles away and then the vast farms that surrounded this town.

The higher he climbed, the more he saw of the world—until he reached the peak. There, standing at the summit, he saw not only the eastern panorama that had unfolded on his way to the top, but also a whole new vista that stretched far into the west.

Sometimes in life our eyes get stuck on the same view. We may see our little corner of the world—and not much else. We may master a portion of the world's vast knowledge, but then become complacent with what little we know. We may glimpse the spiritual and sublime, but then see no need to increase our faith and hope.

There is so much to see, so much to learn, so much to comprehend. Yet, we become focused on a particular point in the path of life and thereby limit our vision.

One wise observer wrote: "Imagine people who look upon the world and see it only in the shades of . . . a black-and-white TV. They will be bewildered by the excitement of others in their midst who see the world in color. It may seem that they live in the same world, that they are seeing the same things. But to [those who see only gray], those who go on and on about the lusciousness of that red rose seem fools."[1]

As we work to see the world in all its glory and grandeur, we find ourselves moving beyond prejudices, beyond hasty judg-ments, beyond misperceptions and misinterpretations. We see beyond ourselves and view others with greater clarity. We are less inclined to fall back on biases and, instead, search for wisdom and learning.

Each of us is capable of seeing more broadly than we do. We may need to climb higher or even take a different direction than what we've grown accustomed to. But as we polish our opinions, seek patiently for greater insights, and open ourselves to ideas that have been beyond our view, we will begin to see the fullness and completeness of truth.

1. Andrew Bard Schmookler, *Fool's Gold: The Fate of Values in a World of Goods* (New York City: HarperCollins, 1993), 4.

Honoring Our Own Old Age

NATIONS ACROSS THE WORLD teach their young to honor their elderly, but, to those who look in the mirror and see an older per-son looking back at them, comes the question: Are you honoring yourself as you grow old?

One writer said, "Let us respect gray hairs, especially our own."[1] To some, growing old is a curse; to others, it is a blessing. What makes the difference? Perhaps it's the perspective of the one doing the growing. Some athletes fear growing older because their bodies cease to perform at the level needed to excel. Some sur-geons experience similar fears as their once steady, dependable hands become shaky and more difficult to control. There is no question that our bodies change as we progress through mortal time. However, that very change may lead us to the most fulfilling experiences life holds for us. There can be great excitement in the venture of new opportunities that age opens up; for no matter how old our bodies may be or feel, we are still able to tap into our great and growing reservoir of knowledge and wisdom and use it to bless mankind.

Research reveals that "nearly two-thirds of all the greatest deeds ever performed by human beings—the victories in battle, the greatest books, the greatest pictures and statues—have been accomplished after the age of sixty."[2]

Most of our senior citizens may be pleasantly surprised to discover that they are already enriching the lives of many as they pursue a dream they never had time for before or as they endure serious health problems with dignity and faith. And consider the immeasurable impact they can have as they listen to and love a child or anyone in need of a friend.

Old age, when lived with wisdom and love, becomes a great blessing to the one in the aging process and to every life it touches. The poet summed it up when he said: "How beautifully the leaves grow old. How full of light and colour are their last days."[3] As we venture into the newness of growing old, we can then smile back at the image in the mirror and honor this sacred time of life.

1. J. P. Senn, in *Barnes and Noble Book of Quotations* (New York City: Barnes and Noble Books, 1987), 21.
2. Albert Edward Wiggam, in *The Christian Leaders Golden Treasury* (Indianapolis: Droke House, 1955), 10.
3. John Burroughs, in *Barnes and Noble Book of Quotations,* 22.

Learning to Say Good-bye

Life teaches us some of its most important lessons by forcing us to learn to say good-bye. At almost every stage of mortality, the nature of life itself causes us to move ahead—sometimes without the people, the places, and the capacities we once enjoyed. Because such events are inevitable for all of us, we must develop the faith and the fortitude to be stretched and strengthened each time life asks us to say good-bye.

Some of life's good-byes are joyous graduations. From childhood, changes come as we leave behind the simple and the familiar to accept new responsibilities and opportunities.

Other ways in which life teaches us to say good-bye are more painful, because they require us to give up a part of ourselves. Over time, we learn that age, illness, or circumstances can force us to abandon activities that were once very important to us. At times we may even struggle to complete tasks that we once accomplished with ease.

Of all the many ways life compels us to say good-bye, the most difficult may be when someone close to us passes away.

In all of life's trials and transitions, it may help to remember that the expression "good-bye" is actually a contraction of the phrase "God be with you."[1] And in all life's good-byes, God will be with us. His timetable may not always seem convenient to us, with our limited perspective. His objectives may not always be clear, but we may rest assured that, through God's mercy and power, our good-byes will not last forever.

Our Father in Heaven is not the God of good-byes but the God of reunion, rejoicing, and life everlasting. He will help us through the turning seasons of life until the promised day arrives when He will reunite "friends on earth and friends above," when all that was lost will be found, and when death and good-bye will be swallowed up in His everlasting love.

---

1. John Ayto, *Dictionary of Word Origins* (New York City: Little, Brown, and Company, 1990), 259.

· LOVE ·

The Arms of Love

SINCE 1968 THE INTERNATIONAL Special Olympics program has provided opportunities for competition and growth to millions of mentally and physically challenged individuals in more than 150 countries. The emphasis of the program is participation, not winning. This idea is stressed by having volunteers who congratulate each athlete after every event. These unselfish volunteers, sometimes referred to as "huggers," encourage the participants throughout the race and wait with loving arms to embrace the athletes just beyond the finish line.

These days, all of us could use a good hugger. As the world has become increasingly competitive and intolerant, we have all experienced feelings of loneliness, depression, and inadequacy. It is easy to wonder if anyone sees our struggles or cares about our challenges. At times we may even hesitate to ask for help, frightened that no one will answer if we call.

At any age, the human heart seeks acceptance, not criticism. Along life's journey toward our mutual destination, we all prefer companions to competitors. And amidst the struggles along the way, we each long to be encircled by loving and understanding arms. As complex and challenging as our lives have become, it is easy to see that the human race often has too many judges, too many spectators, and not nearly enough huggers.

There is within each of us the ability to reach out and improve the world. Our arms are capable of making today better for someone, if only by offering others the little things that make life worth living. Children and grandchildren can be reminded that our love for them is not based on appearance or performance. Coworkers can be complimented and encouraged. Friends can be remembered more frequently and cherished more often. And we can make time for our families. No matter how busy our schedule, we have time to listen, time to laugh, and time to hold each other just a little longer.

Of all God's gifts to us, one of the greatest is the ability to love others more than we love ourselves. Great experiences await us as we put our own cares aside, shunning the spotlight to stand in the shadows and encourage the efforts of another. As we do, our souls and their hearts are forever changed—inseparably linked by the irresistible fusion of unconditional love.

While at times we may feel like the once-wayward prodigal returning to his father's house, we must also remember that each day brings new opportunities to welcome others home, sharing their sorrows and celebrating their achievements. Despite the struggles we may face in life's daily race, we can each rely on the beautiful promise that one day we will cross mortality's finish line and be held in the Arms of Love.

Love Was Present in a Passerby

The essence of the Lord's teaching is to "love thy neighbor." And when asked, "Who is my neighbour?"[1] Christ responded with one of the best-known parables in all of holy writ—the story of the good Samaritan. Alluding to this timeless treasure, Leo Tolstoy writes a short story called "Love" about another poor wayfarer who is rescued, clothed, fed, and sheltered. This grateful traveler recounts his experience and shares some parting wisdom: "I remained alive . . . not by care of myself, but because love was present in a passerby."[2]

While few of us have had an encounter of this magnitude, we can all remember an occasion when "love was present in a passerby." Perhaps an unknown friend shared some change; a compassionate hand held the door; an empathetic voice heard our complaint; or an observant driver stopped to help. Whether the favor was great or small, we remember it and want to be able to return—or at least acknowledge—it. Letters to the editor include frequent attempts to thank a passerby who gave us assistance without giving a name.

In the tradition of the good Samaritan, so many put aside pressing concerns and surmount personal barriers or beliefs to assist a neighbor in need. Without promise of reward or compensation, without prior or pending connection, good men and women continue to help each other. Reservoirs of compassion stand ready to rejuvenate; wellsprings of love come forth to meet a need.

How often do we cross paths with a poor wayfarer—perhaps without even knowing it—who hangs on to the positive word we share, who looks for the smile we wear, who lives by the love we emulate. The Lord, whose love is present for all who pass by, summarized with His life and teachings that "inasmuch as ye have done it unto one of the least of these, . . . ye have done it unto me."[3]

The significance of such selfless deeds is affirmed in a poem about a young man who saved another's life, not with food, clothing, or shelter, but with a passing word of hope and love:

> A nameless man, amid the crowd
> That thronged the daily mart,

Let fall a word of hope and love,
Unstudied from the heart, . . .

It raised a brother from the dust,
It saved a soul from death. . . .

O word of love!
O thought at random cast!
Ye were but little at the first,
But mighty at the last.[4]

1. *New Testament,* Luke 10:29.
2. Leo Tolstoy, "Love," *The Works of Tolstoy* (Roslyn, New York: Black's Readers Service, 1923), 18.
3. *New Testament,* Matthew 25:40.
4. Charles MacKay, "Song of Life," in *The Book of Virtues,* comp. William J. Bennett (New York City: Simon & Schuster, 1993), 142–43.

A Solution to Loneliness

FEELING ALONE IS AMONG the hardest burdens we ever have to bear. Fortunately, there is a reliable solution to this problem—if we have the will to apply it.

One widow felt the sorrow of living alone, even though her grown children came to dinner every Sunday. On these visits the woman would recount her aches and pains, as well as other complaints ranging from bad weather to high prices. One day, however, a neighbor asked the woman to do volunteer work in the local care center for the mentally handicapped. And so the widow began to spend a few hours each week performing simple services—walking in the sunshine with a child in her arms or sitting in a rocker, singing lullabies.

Soon the Sunday visits with her family changed. The mother

no longer seemed interested in talking about her own difficulties; instead, she shared stories of the handicapped children and their parents. She showed the socks and sweaters she was knitting, the cloth dolls she was making, and tried out the new songs she was learning. Her sons and daughters realized that their mother was receiving joy and love in direct proportion to the love and comfort she was giving.

In another time and place, a young man immigrated from Germany to the United States, leaving behind his wife and two small sons until he could earn their passage. Fortunately, he found good work as a railroad engineer. He put in long hours driving a freight train hundreds of miles each day. But his work left no time to become acquainted with others, and he felt deeply lonely, longing for his family. One day he noticed a small boy atop a fence watching the train as it passed. The engineer raised his hand in greeting. The excited boy stood tall on the fence and waved his cap in return. The next day, at the same time, the boy was there again—this time with a playmate. Soon the engineer had five or six young lads waiting for him at various places along the route. Even though they never met, the lonely immigrant father and the admiring young boys shared a friendship that enriched them all.

The widow and the young father had each felt lonely and bereft of love. They solved their problems by finding others to whom they could give love. No matter how alone we may feel, there are always others who need love and support. We have only to lift our eyes from our own loneliness, look around us, and see the ways we can offer love from our hearts. Giving love makes us feel less alone in the world and unites us with God himself, the Author of Love.

· MEMORIES ·

Memories

OF ALL THE CONSOLATIONS OF OUR declining years, perhaps the most comforting are the joyful memories of friends and family past. Watch a chance meeting between former neighbors and see the conversation blossom. Watch a family preparing to move to a new home and see the loving care lavished on the photo albums or the family Bible. The simple phrase "Do you remember . . . ?" has probably led to more delightful discussions among former companions or relatives than any other phrase.

The urge to cling to our memories, to preserve our fondest recollections, expresses itself in a myriad of ways. We keep journals and diaries. We take cameras with us on every family outing, and we are careful to record every birthday on film. Parents, meeting a grown child's new fiancé, welcome their prospective in-law to the family with evenings filled with old color slides or family movies. Images of the past are greeted with shouts of joyful laughter and bursts of story-telling and anecdotes. And evenings full of reminiscences are themselves later recalled with a kind of tranquil delight.

Happy, shared memories can lighten the darkest hour and cheer us when we are at our most despairing. As John Keats put it: "A thing of beauty is a joy for ever: its loveliness increases;

glories infinite haunt us till they become a cheering light unto our souls, and bound to us so fast that, whether there be shine, or gloom o'ercast, they always must be with us."[1]

While not all our memories are "glories infinite," we have the capacity to choose which memories will be our companions and our guides and which we'll allow to fade and wither. And, as we contemplate a good deed done, a charitable impulse followed, the solemn sweetness of a child's conversation, or the modest pleasure of an accomplishment noticed, we restore our souls, re-energize our spirits.

Let our memories be guided by one simple truth: Our spirits live where our minds choose to dwell. Let us choose those memories that enrich and enliven us—that give us comfort and peace.

1. John Keats, "Endymion," in *Confucius to Cummings: an Anthology of Poetry*, ed. Ezra Pound and Marcella Spann (New York City: New Directions, 1964), 221.

The Treasure Trove of Memories

Taking time to preserve and pass on our recollections, our feelings, and our insights can create treasure troves of invaluable memories.

Some 2,000 years ago, Cicero observed that memory is the treasury and guardian of all things.[1] But in our much more modern world, we sometimes fall into the "thick of thin things"[2] and become mentally sidetracked by the busyness of our lives. We lose track of important events, of lessons we should recognize, of quiet stirrings that could serve to strengthen our souls.

As we take time for reflection—as we look for the significant in our lives—we'll find we have much worth remembering. It may be that, when faced with a challenge, we should look beyond the immediate distress and see a lesson worth learning. Or it may be that a casual exchange with a child or grandchild carries meaning that can only be seen with a moment's pause. Whether systematically at the end of the day or more sporadically, when we can find a spare minute, time taken to contemplate and meditate can teach us much.

We then would be wise to keep a record of some sort—whether it be a more formal diary or random notes that we will one day gather together. For without some means of recording that which is worth remembering, we too often find that memories fade all too fast.

Finally, there is value in sharing our lives with others. Families grow closer as they tell of their days at dinnertime. Friendships are strengthened as we remember together times both happy and sad. Whatever the setting, as we share our memories, we strengthen our ties.

In preserving the story of his life, the writer Russell Baker observed, "We all come from the past, and [we] ought to know . . . that life is a braided cord of humanity stretching up from time long ago."[3]

As we gather together and then share the moments of our lives we will add our memories to the braided cords of family and friends.

1. H. L. Mencken, ed., *A New Dictionary of Quotations* (New York City: Alfred A. Knopf, 1985), 777.
2. Edith Wharton, as quoted by Jeffrey R. Holland, "The Bond of Charity" (Provo, Utah: BYU Annual University Conference Proceedings, 1980), 6.
3. Russell Baker, *Growing Up* (New York City: Plume Books, 1982), 8.

Making Memories in Time

AMONG THE RESOURCES WE EACH POSSESS, our time is the most precious and perishable. Each day ticking clocks and changing calendars, growing children and aging parents, remind us that life is fragile and fleeting. When we were children, it seemed like an endless procession of days would give us more than enough time to do everything; as adults, we realize that our limited time forces us to make important decisions and to create priorities. Still, too easily and too often we squander our time, forgetting that "time is the stuff of which life is made."[1]

Time is truly a unique commodity; it can be exchanged for almost anything. However, since time cannot be stored, reused, or borrowed, it is the one particular in which all of us are equal. Each morning we receive another 24 hours of life to invest, with the promise that we each will become a living record of what we choose to do with our time.

We cannot waste time without bruising eternity. Instead of making memories, we are too frequently waiting to live—promising ourselves that after graduation, when the children are grown, or after we retire, we will then live life as we've dreamed it. How we wish to relive our wasted hours if at life's end we discover, in the poet's words, "I have spent my life stringing and unstringing my instrument and all the while the song I had meant to sing has been left unsung."[2]

While time's unfaltering cadence beats on, every day that is well lived rewards us with beautiful echoes of time we call memories. God has given each of us the gift of time, and while we live, our lives are like unfinished symphonies. Each day offers us the chance to add a new measure, to revise part of the melody, or even to erase a few discordant notes. And when we learn, as Kipling expressed it, to "fill each unforgiving minute with sixty seconds worth of distance run,"[3] time becomes the treasure it was intended to be.

Each morning God offers us another 24 hours; each evening we can consider how another day of our life was spent. When we use our time wisely, treasuring each day as if it were our last, we find that "yesterday is but a dream, and tomorrow is only a vision, but today well lived, makes yesterday a dream of happiness and every tomorrow a vision of hope."[4]

1. Benjamin Franklin, *The Way to Wealth*, 17 July 1747.
2. Rabindranath Tagore, in *May Peace Be with You* (Salt Lake City: Deseret Book Company, 1994), 11.
3. Rudyard Kipling, "If," in *One Hundred and One Famous Poems*, ed. Roy J. Cook (Chicago: Contemporary Books, Inc., 1958), 113.
4. Ancient Sanskrit, as quoted in Robert Barlow Fox, *Color the Wind* (Hanover: Christopher Publishing House, 1995), prologue.

· MUSIC ·

The Gentle Power of Music

AT TIMES, WHEN IN THE MIDST OF DESPAIR or discouragement, we long for some experience that will lift our spirits beyond ourselves and give us feelings of hope and peace. We need not search far for such an occasion, for these feelings can be distilled upon us almost instantly through the power of music. It was Thomas Carlyle who said, "Music is well said to be the speech of angels."[1] It has the power to speak not only to our minds but also to our hearts.

We are surrounded with opportunities to enjoy every variety of uplifting and inspiring music. Musical artists perform in great and small halls throughout the world. Their performances enrich our lives whenever we are able to attend such events. Also, consider the rich rewards of attending a concert at a school, where young singers, well-taught by a devoted conductor, sing their songs of enthusiasm. It can have an almost magical effect on an audience, causing the troubles of the world to move aside as we walk in the sunlight of life for that moment. This contagious feeling is also evident when we hear a band playing spirited marches in a parade or at a ballgame. Trumpets, flutes, cymbals, drums— all come together in a grand harmonious proclamation of optimism. And our spirits are lifted.

John Dryden said, "What passion cannot music raise and

quell?"[2] The answer was evident on a battlefield at the edge of Paris in 1870 on Christmas Eve. In the heat of the Franco-Prussian War, one young Frenchman jumped suddenly from his trench and began to sing "O Holy Night." His beautiful tenor voice filled the air with peace, and all fighting ceased as he sang. When he had finished, immediately from the other side a tall German arose from his trench and responded by singing Martin Luther's beloved carol, "Vom Himmel Hoch"—"From Heaven on High."[3] On that sacred night, music had the power to halt a war.

Music can also restore or enhance romance in a marriage as couples listen together to the songs that touched them during the days of their courtship. As tender harmonies are heard, hearts are once again united.

Music has the power not only to renew love but also to comfort the afflicted. That became evident when a little child, flushed with fever, snuggled in his mother's arms and faintly asked, "Please sing me a song."

Finally, and perhaps most significant of all, through the majesty of music we can honor our divine Creator by singing praises to Him. It was Isaiah who wrote, "Sing, O ye heavens; for the Lord hath done it: . . . break forth in singing, ye mountains."[4] As we sing our anthems of praise, perhaps even the angels, whose language it is, may join us in the singing as we feel the touch of heaven upon us.

1. Thomas Carlyle, in *The Harper Book of Quotations* (New York City: HarperPerennial, 1993), 312.
2. John Dryden, in *LDS Collectors Library: Famous Quotes*, CD-ROM (Salt Lake City: Infobases, Inc., 1993).
3. Joy Saunders Lundberg and Janice Kapp Perry, *Christmas, A Carol Cantata* (Orem, Utah: Jackman Music Corp., 1981), 11, 12, 16.
4. *Old Testament*, Isaiah 44:23.

Songs of the Heart

INTERTWINED WITH OUR VERY EXISTENCE are experiences with the wonder and power of music. As night approaches, a mother's lullaby hushes fretting cries, and a lifetime later, a favorite hymn is sung at the funeral service that signals the close of life's short day. Between birth and death our love and worship, our faith and patriotism, our devotion and praise are all eloquently conveyed by the lyrics and melodies of music. It has been said that we speak with our lips, but to sing we must use our hearts.

Those who have felt deeper peace and greater joy in their lives as the result of singing know the power of music, and who has not felt chills after hearing trained voices and skilled musicians perform in harmonized perfection? Unfortunate is the individual who has not experienced what T. S. Eliot describes as "music heard so deeply that it is not heard at all, but you are the music while the music lasts."[1]

Unfortunately, not all music is uplifting and not all lyrics are enlightening. We must carefully choose, for music can plant thoughts deeper into our minds and hearts than words alone. The music we select shapes our perceptions, alters our attitudes, and influences our lifestyles.

As human beings, our greatest joys and deepest pains are expressed in our music. Is it any wonder the Lord has stated, "The song of the righteous is a prayer unto me"?[2] Our days are brighter when we choose to whistle a happy tune or to hum the melody of a comforting hymn during times of temptation or trial. Music is a gift from God; even the simplest song of praise is heard in the heavens, because the majesty on high is both our origin and our destiny.

Shortly before his death, John Donne penned these words: "Since I am coming to that holy room, where with thy choir of saints forever more, I shall be made thy music; as I come I tune the instrument here at the door."[3]

The power of music influences the lives of individuals and the destinies of nations. Whether we sing or listen with our hearts, music spans barriers of language and time to knit human hearts together in common experience and mutual devotion. Music's power to bless our lives is not based on musical talent, but on our ability to feel and believe. When our songs express the true feelings of our souls, they are songs of the heart; for when our souls reverberate with the strains of beautiful music, our hearts truly sing and we commune with our fellowmen and with God.

1. T. S. Eliot, "The Dry Salvages V," *Collected Poems* 1909–1962 (New York City: Harcourt, Brace, Jovanovich, 1971), 199.

2. *Doctrine and Covenants* 25:12.

3. John Donne, "Hymn to God My God, in My Sickness," in *Major Poets of the Earlier Seventeenth Century,* ed. Barbara K. Lewalski and Andrew J. Sabol (New York City: The Odyssey Press, 1973), 169.

Lift Up Your Voice and Sing

THROUGHOUT THE WORLD, music fills the air. Nowhere is there a civilization devoid of song, a culture without its own unique style of musical expression. Music paints a portrait of each society; it weaves a rich tapestry, depicting for listeners what we fear, what we love, and what we believe in.

Mothers everywhere sing lullabies to their children. Warriors and soldiers rally to drum beats and marching songs. Eyes moisten at the singing of national anthems. Hearts quicken and memories awaken as we hear the songs that played as we fell in love.

Music helps us communicate our feelings. As one music professor said: "Something we cannot say, we can often sing. And music can help us express a feeling for which we have no words. Music is the natural outcome of feeling."[1]

Music has power. It can bring comfort when we sorrow, peace when we are afraid. It can inspire us to greater good and evoke reverence for that which is holy. It can elicit feelings of joy, patriotism, triumph, romance, and love.

The faint humming of "Silent Night" by a lone soldier during World War II unified enemies in their foxholes one cold Christmas Eve. A few familiar notes brought the day's fighting to a close and reminded all those on the battlefield that, beneath their differences, they were united by a common faith in God.

On another occasion, religious hymns hummed quietly behind the Iron Curtain helped believers gather in safety, united by inspiring chords of praise to the Creator.

And Christ himself sang a hymn just prior to his crucifixion as we read in Mark, "And when they had sung an hymn, they went out into the Mount of Olives."[2]

Words alone have impact upon our ears, but set to music, they can penetrate our hearts. Pity the soul who never takes the opportunity to rejoice in beautiful music. What a monumental loss; what a missed opportunity!

And what of those who never sing? Is this not tragic, also? Never mind whether or not you were blessed with a glorious singing voice. Is there a child in the world who doesn't love to hear his mother or father sing, regardless of their expertise? A song that truly comes from the heart is beautiful by any standards.

To raise one's voice in song is a form of worship; it is an act of love that transcends quality of performance. Dozens of times throughout the Bible, we are admonished to praise the Lord in song. Nowhere does it say that our voices must be perfect. Let us all take advantage of the opportunity to sing. Our hearts will gladden, our spirits will rejoice, and our souls will grow as we lift up our voice and sing.

---

1. Dr. John Jennings, as quoted in Sue Van Alfen, "Singing the Songs We Love, Loving the Songs We Sing," *Ensign,* Jan. 1978, 34.
2. *New Testament,* Mark 14:26.

· PATRIOTISM ·

Love of Country

LOVE OF COUNTRY CAN BRING great joy to living. Such love implies more than passion or sentiment; love means action. Indeed, if we truly love our land, we take part in making it better. We uphold its virtues. We learn its history. We volunteer.

Theodore Roosevelt, the twenty-sixth President of the United States, understood the value of serving his country. Eighty years ago, just before his death, he explained love of country this way: [It] means the virtues of courage, honor, justice, truth, sincerity, and hardihood." And then he cautioned against those things that destroy such patriotism: "Prosperity-at-any-price, peace-at-any-price, safety-first instead of duty-first, the love of soft living and the get-rich-quick theory of life."[1] In other words, real love of country demands something of us. It requires commitment to ideals and willingness to work hard for them.

While the contributions we make to our countries and communities may not be memorialized with statues on town squares, they are significant nonetheless. Consider the patriots—past and present—who serve in the armed forces, sometimes giving their lives for freedom. Certainly, they demonstrate love of country.

And yet, day in and day out across this and other lands, people serve their country in many other ways. As they contribute,

115

they come to have deep feelings of love for the land they serve. One woman picks up the litter she sees along the path of her morning walk. Not only does it make the city more beautiful, but it also makes her happy all day.

On national holidays some Boy Scouts place flags on the front lawns of elderly or disabled residents. The flags they raise enliven the homebound and remind all who pass of the importance of the day.

Other responsible citizens attend town meetings. They become informed voters; they uphold the laws of the land.

As good citizens, they show their love of country by looking out for neighbors—whether across the street or around the world. Their land becomes "the grandest on earth," the land that they love, because they do their part to make it better.

---

1. Theodore Roosevelt, *Respectfully Quoted: A Dictionary of Quotations Requested from the Congressional Research Service*, ed. Suzy Platt (Washington, D.C.: Library of Congress, 1989), 22.

"For Patriot's Dream"

A FRAIL MAN LEANS ON HIS CANE, hobbling one careful step at a time. Impatiently, shoppers push past him, eager to resume their lively stride. Little do these passers-by realize who this man is. He is one of millions who were crippled while fighting valiantly for our freedom, a veteran of war. If only we knew what he had done for us, we might not brush past him so quickly. We might pause a moment to remember his contribution—the life he was willing to give that all of us may live in peace.

So many blessings are ours today because of sacrifices made by someone else. Countless numbers of servicemen and servicewomen have given their lives and forfeited their futures, paying the ultimate price for the freedoms we enjoy.

It is a gift they have given us freely, yet it's a hard one to repay. We can only try to show our gratitude and the honor we feel for these noble heroes by our daily efforts to cherish the land they preserved and the people who made it possible.

As citizens of this great nation, we can take steps to ensure that these valiant soldiers did not give their lives in vain. We can safeguard our laws and freedoms, electing the best among us to sit in our seats of government. We can teach love of country to our children and instill in them a determination to keep our flag waving proudly.

We can study the issues, campaign for righteous causes, and support those we believe in.

Some of our brothers and sisters in countries around the world are breathing the sweet air of freedom for the very first time. How dear these liberties are, and how vital it is that we work to make certain those freedoms are never lost. Too many have fought too hard and for too long for us to forget the debt we owe. Wherever we are, we can rejoice in those liberties and make efforts to protect our blessings and stability.

And as we do, our lives will take on a new gleam—the shine of peace and the radiance that comes when we set our personal problems aside and work for the good of mankind. May freedom ever light our way.

· P E A C E ·

Peace—a Rare, Yet Sturdy, Flower

OF ALL THE PLANTS THAT GROW in this garden that is our life, none is hardier than peace.

Peace can survive under some of the most difficult situations we know. It can thrive amid poverty. It can flourish where sickness is, or war—and yes, even in the presence of death. Sometimes in the darkest hours, when no light shines, the sweet balm of unseen peace will soothe our souls. We have many moving testimonies of the staying power of peace under the most agonizing conditions.

Yet, hardy as it is, peace is also a rare flower. When we encounter someone filled with peace, we feel ourselves in the presence of someone unusual, possessed of something enviable. The Prophet Isaiah referred to the Messiah as "The Prince of Peace."[1] Peace is perhaps heaven's sweetest gift. When we have inner peace, we can bear any pain or sorrow; when we lack that peace, even our greatest blessings cannot bring us joy or comfort.

How, then, do we nurture this rare and precious flower?

In the political sense, peace means the absence of war. In the spiritual sense, peace is the absence of a divided heart. Peace, as sturdy as it is, cannot flourish when we are at war with ourselves. Even the Prince of Peace cannot grant us the blessing of peace until we ourselves call a truce to our internal civil war. If we preach tolerance and love, yet practice bigotry and hate, peace withers within us. If we believe that our families are more important than any worldly achievement or possession, but spend most of our energies getting and spending, peace cannot ripen and bear its fruit in our lives. A wise rabbi taught his congregation that sin is whatever we cannot do with a whole heart.[2] When we live whole-heartedly—body, mind, and spirit all in harmony—then we have prepared the way to receive the peace of God.

1. *Old Testament*, Isaiah 9:6.
2. Author unknown.

Peace

ONE OF THE GREAT CONTRADICTIONS of history is the sad fact that nearly all people—nearly all places and times—have fervently desired peace while actively engaged in war. Throughout time, men and women have talked of peace, sought for peace, even prayed for peace; but peace always seems to elude us. War itself is often talked of as a prelude to peace; and we're told that, when we win this battle or defeat this enemy, we'll have finally earned a lasting peace. And yet, we find that war leads inexorably to further war, and the phrase "a war to end all wars" remains a sad commentary of all humanity.

But is peace simply an absence of war—something passive and static? Or is peace itself something more active and positive? In the Law of Moses, the children of Israel were commanded to make peace offerings—feasts of celebration and friendship. To them, peace was attained through fellowship. In the Sermon on the Mount, Christ blessed not those who lived in peace, but those who made peace. The Apostle Paul told the Romans that peace was a gift given to him who "worketh good"[1] and urged the Romans to "follow after the things which make for peace."[2]

It is a foolish parent who thinks that "a little peace and quiet" can be gained by shouting at rowdy children to "shut up and leave me alone." The wise parent will cure rowdiness with kindness and attention, replacing bedlam with quiet games or stories.

It is true that the deepest peace we can know is found in solitude and holy communion with our God, but that communion, too, is gained through effort and sacrifice. In His last words to His disciples, the Prince of Peace spoke of the tribulations and difficulties they would soon have to face. He then concluded: "These things I have spoken unto you that *in me* ye might have peace . . . [for] I have overcome the world."[3]

The quarrels and quibbles of men, women, and nations will always be part of mortality. But in the midst of tumult and confusion, it is possible to find peace—a lasting peace, the peace of God.

1. *New Testament,* Romans 2:10.
2. *New Testament,* Romans 14:19.
3. *New Testament,* John 16:33.

"Peace, Be Still"

ONE OF THE MOST UNIVERSAL human pursuits is the quest for personal peace. Regardless of our circumstances, we share a soul-deep desire to know that our lives have purpose, that God is there, and that He loves us. However, striving to be at harmony with ourselves, our fellowmen, and with God can be difficult and discouraging—especially when storms of doubt and tempests of trial buffet our lives.

There may be times when we, like the disciples of old, feel

abandoned to the waves. Although the Master Himself slept in the stern of their ship, they despaired and cried to Him: "Carest thou not that we perish?"[1] The same feelings reverberate through our own lives when our challenges seem greater than our resources or when circumstances and setbacks fill our hearts with anger or anguish. And yet, the Master is there.

Though the world will always be a place of turmoil, strife, and injustices, the Lord's promise is that we can have peace in spite of external events. He has assured us that He will not forget us nor forsake us; and when we trust in Him, peace can come.

Peace comes from knowing—knowing we are living our lives in harmony with all the truth we have. In a world that teaches relativism and situational ethics, there is great comfort and lasting power in living our lives in obedience to principles and commandments that are fixed, sure, and constant. We cannot expect to feel right if we continue to walk in paths that we know are wrong.

Peace also comes from remembering—remembering we can forgive and be forgiven. Each day offers new opportunities to live in peace. Old grudges can be forgotten. Instances where others have hurt or offended us can be forgiven. And continual introspection can give us new perspective on how we can change our lives for the better. We cannot expect our hearts to be filled with joy and peace until we have purged them of bitterness and regret.

And peace comes from believing—believing in the midst of a weary and war-torn world, where insensitivity and chaos reign, that the Prince of Peace can still establish His kingdom in humble hearts that ache for peace. For those who seek Him, the Master's gentle voice can still be heard, bringing peace even in the midst of life's raging storms: "Peace, be still." His promises are sure, and there is not a tempest that His words cannot calm.

---

1. *New Testament,* Mark 4:37–38.

"Let There Be Peace"

Peace is the state of being that all mankind longs for. Wars are fought to secure it, songs are written to inspire it, and prayers are petitioned to obtain it. We all want peace. Most of us can do little to bring about global peace, but we can do everything to bring about our own personal peace.

What is peace? Webster defines it as "freedom from disagreement or quarrels . . . [the] absence of mental conflict . . . [a state of] tranquility, serenity."[1] If we are not experiencing tranquility and serenity in our lives, we would do well to examine why not. Often, the loss of peace comes from small, insignificant disagreements with those closest to us—particularly our neighbors and family members.

One man, upon examining his own lack of peace, decided it was time to heal a long-standing conflict with his next-door neighbor. He said, "We had battled over such foolish things as his barking dog, my out-of-control sprinklers, his falling fruit littering my lawn—and on it went." He continued: "One day, I decided the feud had gone on long enough. I took a large pork roast from my freezer and went to his home. When he answered the door, I said: 'It's time for us to have peace. Forgive me for all my unkindness to you, and please accept this gift as a peace offering.'" With that simple gesture, the feud was over and a peaceful relationship began. We each have the power to bring about tranquility in our neighborhoods.

And what about our homes? Are there angry conflicts that have been festering for months, even years, with a child, a parent, an in-law? It's good to remember that "anger doesn't solve anything. It builds nothing, but can destroy everything."[2] Most certainly, it will destroy peace. Some prefer to stubbornly blame others and refuse to recognize their own contribution to domestic conflicts. It seems they would rather be right at all cost. Often, when one initiates an apology, the other follows and peace is restored. Thomas S. Monson said, "Truly peace will reign triumphant when we improve ourselves after the pattern taught by the Lord."[3]

There is no question—we are responsible for our own personal peace. It takes effort and sincere willingness and pays such big dividends. What a peaceful world this would be if each of us believed that we can play a significant role in bringing peace into the world.

---

1. *Webster's New World Dictionary,* 2nd college edition (Englewood Cliffs, New Jersey: Prentice-Hall, 1970), 1044.
2. L. Douglas Wilder, in *Deseret News,* 1 December 1991, A2.
3. Thomas S. Monson, "The Path to Peace," *Ensign,* May 1994, 62.

A Prayer for Peace

AMONG THE NATIONS OF THE WORLD, no worthy achievement has proved more challenging or elusive than the quest for lasting peace.

History records few years unmarred by the ravages of war. And so, men and women everywhere endlessly express the ancient prophet's prayer that "nation shall not lift up a sword against nation, neither shall they learn war any more."[1]

Nevertheless, wars rage on across the world. Perhaps the time has finally come for us to appreciate the insight of Elie Wiesel, when he said: "Mankind must remember that peace is not God's gift to his creatures; peace is our gift to each other."[2]

In other words, peace is your responsibility—and mine. We may pray for peace, but we must also practice peace.

St. Augustine observed that "two cities have been formed by two loves: the earthly by the love of self . . . ; the heavenly by the love of God."[3]

Too often, the earthly city—the city of man—is made up of those motivated by unbridled greed, by a lust for power, by corrupt aims and ambitions.

On the other hand, the city of God will only be established as we accept and apply a simple formula revealed by great religious leaders and philosophers throughout the history of the world.

In the sixth century B.C., Confucius said: "What you don't want done to yourself, don't do to others."[4]

A thousand years later, Buddha taught his followers to "Hurt not others with that which pains thyself."[5]

Plato said, "May I do to others as I would that they should do unto me."[6]

And Jesus of Nazareth advised, "Whatsoever you would that men should do to you, do ye even so to them."[7]

The Golden Rule—expressed in different words perhaps, but providing through the ages an enduring and profound pattern for peace. The Golden Rule implies that peace begins not with nations, but with individuals—with you and with me.

As Thomas à Kempis wrote: "First keep the peace within yourself; then you can also bring peace to others."[8]

The dictionary describes peace not only as "freedom from war," but also as "freedom from disagreement or quarrels," and as "an undisturbed state of mind."[9]

By those definitions, you and I can achieve peace—and so can he and she and they.

"Peace is a journey of a thousand miles," said Lyndon Johnson, "and it must be taken one step at a time."[10]

You can take one step today. I can take another step tomorrow. Together, each of us—in our own small way—can, as the *Bible* advises, "seek peace, and pursue it"[11]; for "Blessed are the peacemakers. . . . They shall be called the children of God."[12]

---

1. *Old Testament:* Micah 4:3.

2. Elie Wiesel, in *Simpson's Contemporary Quotations* (Boston: Houghton Mifflin, 1988), 245.

3. St Augustine, in *Bartlett's Familiar Quotations,* 16th edition, ed. Justin Kaplan (Boston: Little, Brown and Company, 1982), 115.

4. Confucius, *Constructing a Life Philosophy,* ed. David L. Bender (San Diego: Greenhaven Press, 1993), 159.

5. Ibid.

6. Ibid.

7. *New Testament,* Matthew 7:12.

8. Thomas à Kempis, in *Bartlett's Familiar Quotations,* 15th edition, ed. John Bartlett (Boston: Little, Brown and Company, 1980), 148.

9. *Webster's New World Dictionary,* 3rd college ed. (New York City: Simon and Schuster, 1988), 993.

10. *Speechwriter's Newsletter,* published by Ragan Communications, Inc., Chicago, 8 April 1994, 5.

11. *Old Testament,* Psalm 34:14.

12. *New Testament,* Matthew 5:9.

· SELF-WORTH ·

Recognizing Our Own Self-Worth

T HE DISCOVERY OF OUR OWN individual worth and who we really are is one of the most significant discoveries we can make in our lifetime. Erich Fromm said, "*Integrity* simply means a willingness not to violate one's identity."[1] Knowing our identity, then, becomes a primary need. So, who are we? The scriptures testify that we are literally children of God, a loving Father in Heaven. Understanding that we are made in His "image and after [His] likeness"[2] can powerfully affect our lives for good. We all understand to some degree how we inherit certain qualities and tendencies from our mortal parents; however, we often fail to realize that this same principle applies with our Heavenly Father. Within us, we possess His qualities of goodness, His divine nature.

Have you ever cut an apple open across the middle instead of cutting it lengthwise, as we traditionally do? If you have, you know that inside of every apple, regardless of bruises and deformities on the outside, there is a perfect star. If we could look inside ourselves, we could make that equally surprising discovery and find that we, too, have a beautiful inner self. It is that beauty within—that divine nature, the star within us, if you will—that empowers us to achieve our greatest potential.

To recognize our own individual worth and value is not

arrogance nor vanity. It is a form of Godlike love in action. It is through this recognition that we are able to develop our inborn divine qualities, which then empowers us to reach out and help others recognize their worth. To notice and emulate the best traits of our earthly parents is one of the highest tributes we can pay them. So it is when we see in ourselves our true identity as one of God's children and do our best to emulate His ways that we pay Him the highest honor and respect possible.

That does not mean we must expect to be perfect. We are human and we make mistakes. That's when we need to remember that one of the divine attributes of God is to forgive, and that includes forgiving ourselves and then pressing forward with a steadfastness in our effort to be more like Him. Each of us, no matter our condition in life, is capable of this goal—a goal whose journey brings us personal peace. Russell M. Nelson said, "We are sons and daughters of God, He is our Father; we are his children. Our divine inheritance is the magnificence of man."[3] Today, as you look in the mirror, take a minute; discover the star inside of you and recognize who you really are—a divinely created being who has a loving Father in Heaven.

1. Erich Fromm, in *Barnes and Noble Book of Quotations* (New York City: Harper & Row, 1987), 323.
2. *Old Testament*, Genesis 1:26–27.
3. Russell M. Nelson, *The Power within Us* (Salt Lake City: Deseret Book Company, 1988), 14.

Looking toward the Stars

As LONG AS MANKIND HAS INHABITED this earth, the night skies have served as a source of inspiration for shepherds, for sailors, for explorers—for all who have stood in awe before the immensity of space.

There have been those who have charted their courses across seemingly endless oceans by studying the heavens, while others have seen significance in the patterns formed by stars visible from their own backyards. Some have dreamed of discoveries waiting to be made, while others have sought to connect with the eternal implications of a frontier that knows no bounds. Some have been mystified by the depths of the night's sky, while others have found comfort and calm as they have felt a connection with the eternal nature of the universe.

As we look into an expanse that is without beginning or end, we sense something of our own eternal nature. As we contemplate the insights that have been gained into the nature of galaxies the naked eye cannot even see, we find assurance that the unknown can become known. And as we discover the grand designs that finite minds can scarcely comprehend, we realize that we, too, are part of a greater whole which is guided by a loving God who governs the universe.

In the silence of the night, as one looks out into the heavens, this simple sentence by Emerson suggests at least one lesson that can be drawn from such a sight. Said he, "All I have seen teaches me to trust the Creator for all I have not seen."[1]

There is, indeed, much in the skies beyond what our eyes can see; in fact, as scientists have ever more sophisticated means to explore the heavens, we seem to find, in addition to what can now be seen, just how much we cannot yet comprehend.

One wise physicist, who had studied the mysteries of space for many years, took a small group of interested students away from the city lights late one night and showed them, with the help of a powerful telescope, parts of the universe they had only read about in their books. As his students marvelled at what they saw, he set aside his usual scientific objectivity and shared his deeply held belief that what they were seeing was the work of a divine force. "I do not understand exactly how he has created what he has," the scientist told his students, "but the more I study the heavens, the more convinced I am that we are not here by chance."

Discovering the purposes of our lives—individually and collectively—is a challenging process at best. But sometimes we can learn much about ourselves and our world—and about Him who has given us these gifts—by waiting for the evening to come and then quietly contemplating the handiwork of God.

1. Ralph Waldo Emerson, in Richard L. Evans, *An Open Door* (Salt Lake City: Publishers Press, 1967), 209.

Unlocking Our Divine Potential

THE IMMENSE WORTH OF EACH HUMAN SOUL lies in the almost limitless potential that each of us has to become like God. By planting seeds of greatness within us, our Heavenly Father has invited us to be partners with Him in pursuing all that He knows we can become.

While we are each aware of areas where we have the capacity to be better people, too often we fail to focus and act on these God-given aptitudes and desires. As William James said: "Most people live . . . in a very restricted circle of their potential being. They make use of a very small portion . . . of their soul's resources."[1] If we allow them to, external critics and internal doubts will prevent us from achieving all that we could. Sometimes it seems easier to argue for our limitations than to explore our possibilities.

To reach our potential, we must move beyond our self-imposed limits and past mistakes. As one author noted: "Our deepest fear is not that we are inadequate. Our deepest fear is that we are powerful beyond measure. . . . We ask ourselves, Who am I to be brilliant, gorgeous, talented, and fabulous? Actually, who are you not to be? You are a child of God."[2]

As we grow toward our divine potential, we need to be patient during the seasons of failure and adversity that often precede growth and success. Thomas Edison's potential as an inventor was not demonstrated by the thousands of light bulbs he made that did not work, but by the last one he created that did. Each successive failure that distance runner Roger Bannister had helped prepare him to fulfill his potential to make him the first man ever to run a mile in less than four minutes. And so it is with us.

Through persistence and hard work, we can each unlock the potential God has given us. We have within us not only the capacity to accomplish great things but also the ability to do ordinary things in extraordinary ways. With an abiding faith that God has given us the potential to be more than we are today, our desires to be more patient, more courageous, and more loving will be ultimately realized. "All the hopes that sweetly start from the fountain of the heart"[3] are within our reach if we have the faith and perseverance to realize our God-given potential.

1. William James, in *Bartlett's Familiar Quotations*, 15th edition, ed. John Bartlett (Boston: Little, Brown and Company, 1980), 648.
2. Marianne Williamson, *A Return to Love* (New York City: Harper Collins, 1992), 165.
3. Thomas C. Griggs, "God Is Love," *Hymns of The Church of Jesus Christ of Latter-day Saints* (Salt Lake City: The Church of Jesus Christ of Latter-day Saints, 1985), no. 313.

Rising to the Top

A YOUNG GIRL RAISED ON A DAIRY FARM once heard her father say, "There is cream in all fresh milk. Given a little time, it will rise to the top." She noticed that the cream then became a premium product with a high value. So it is with people. We all have premium qualities within us. Given a little time and effort, our qualities will develop and rise to the top and then we become far more valuable to all humanity.

What is it that causes desirable qualities to develop? It has been said that "there are always choices—two paths to take. One is easy. And its only reward is that it's easy."[1] There is nothing to be gained from ease. It is only through hard work and overcoming challenges that we develop qualities that enrich our lives.

A young couple with three children, recently facing financial difficulties, reported that it is through this adversity they are developing the ability to use their money with greater wisdom. And in the process, they have discovered how much more rewarding it is to give "time" to their children instead of costly "things."

One man, struggling with the loss of his family through divorce, realized that, through the passage of time and with faith in Divine help, he has been able to forgive. And, as a result, he has developed an even closer relationship with his children. Because of his determination to treat his former wife and her husband with kindness during a recent difficult situation, his teenage son hugged him and said: "Thanks, Dad. I knew I could count on you to bring peace."

Some challenges seem almost insurmountable; and yet, qualities of greatness are developed from them. Such was the case with Viktor Frankl as he endured with fortitude and faith the atrocities of concentration camps. He inspired many who struggle when he said, "Everything can be taken from a man but one thing: the last of human freedoms—to choose one's attitude in any given set of circumstances—to choose one's own way."[2]

Yes, like the cream in milk, our God-given qualities will rise to the top as we face life's challenges with faith and courage. It is then that we become of premium value, able to give what really matters and enjoy life to the fullest.

1. Jack Canfield et al., *Chicken Soup for the Teenage Soul* (Deerfield Beach, Florida: Health Communications, Inc., 1997), 97.
2. Viktor Frankl, in *The Harper Book of Quotations* (New York City: HarperCollins, 1993), 256.

Self-Worth

Finding a Niche

ONE OF THE MOST FRUSTRATING, but important, aspects of life's journey can be the search to find our place in this world. We all need to be needed. We want to serve, and we want to feel as though we've made a difference. We all know that we've been given talents, but too often we are at a loss as to how to use them.

Perhaps we set our sights too high—hold ourselves to a standard beyond our capacity. The niche we find for ourselves may not necessarily be in the limelight. A talented basketball player can make a difference on the floor whether or not he or she ever plays professional basketball. A young musician may never become a Mozart, but he or she can still bless the world with the timeless gift of music. Sometimes it's enough to be a friend, listen sympathetically to a troubled heart, or offer encouragement when a neighbor is "having a bad day."

One of the great challenges of parenting can be helping children find their own sense of purpose and hidden talents. A father was near despair over his sullen, uncommunicative teenage son. Day after day the boy sat in his room listening to music and playing endless games on his computer that, to the father, offered little sense of hope or joy. He tried involving his son in sporting activities and other excursions that he himself enjoyed—but to no avail. The boy seemed to have given up completely. Then, one day the father discovered a poem the boy had written. He didn't read much poetry and couldn't understand what his son was trying to communicate. But the wise father realized that perhaps this might be a gift his son could and should develop. Instead of criticism and rejection, he offered words of encouragement and was truly pleased when one of his son's poems was accepted for publication. Although the son's talents and interests were different from his father's, they shared the same need for acceptance and accomplishment.

We owe it to ourselves to discover our talents and to find opportunities to share them. And we owe it to our family, friends, and neighbors to use our abilities in helpful ways. Even when we feel discouraged, lonely, or sometimes useless, we need to remember that God has given each of us great potential. We all have a place in life and in the lives of those we love.

· SERVICE ·

Helping Those in Need

ONE OF THE MOST DIFFICULT DILEMMAS of life can occur when we sense that a loved one or friend needs help, but we're not sure how to provide it. Perhaps we see a child crying. Something has upset her, but when we ask what's wrong, she quickly replies, "Nothing." Maybe a friend has lost his job, and we want to show our support and sympathy. But it is often difficult to find the right words. Perhaps a neighbor has suffered a loss, and we want to provide what comfort we can. But we are also reluctant to intrude inappropriately.

It is easy under such circumstances to feel helpless or inadequate, with little comfort to offer and little joy to share. It is important, however, that we not allow our feelings of discomfort to prevent us from offering what aid we can. Almost always, the help we offer will be gratefully received. Sometimes even a small gesture that says "I care" can be enough to make a difference.

A businessman sat in a busy airport and noticed a young mother struggling with a tired, crying child. At first he was reluctant to intrude. He was, after all, a stranger. Perhaps an offer to help would be resented, he thought. But seeing an edge of desperation on the young woman's face persuaded him to intervene. She responded to his offered help with a grateful thank you. He held her child while she filled a bottle and watched her bags as she changed the baby's diaper. Although his aid lasted only a few minutes and he never saw her again, he had the satisfaction of knowing that he had made a difference and had turned a difficult moment into a manageable one for someone who, however briefly, had needed him.

While we may not always know exactly what to do in times of difficulty, we can almost always help in a small way. And sometimes a small gesture of help, offered sincerely to someone genuinely in need, can literally change a life for the better.

A Tool in God's Hands

A FAMILY WAS TRAVELING ON VACATION, when suddenly their car broke down. The father raised the hood to look at the engine and discovered new parts were needed. Unfortunately, the nearest town was miles away.

Just then another car—also containing several children—pulled up behind them and stopped. The father in that car soon assessed the needs of these strangers and drove to the next town and back to bring the necessary parts.

The stranded family was astonished at such kindness and tried to express their gratitude. But the benevolent stranger waved away their thanks, simply saying, "Every day we pray as a family that the Lord will lead us to people who can use our help." They felt grateful to be used as a tool in God's hands.

What would life be like if we placed ourselves in God's service every day? What if, wherever we went, we looked for people we could assist? Might we find the joy we are all seeking? When we focus upon others, instead of upon ourselves, we magically find that elusive happiness that always escapes the self-centered.

What if, when we prayed, we offered ourselves as tools for God to use in whatever way He needs us? Perhaps we'd be led to those who simply need a comforting word or a listening ear. Or we might discover talents we never knew lay dormant. Meaning and purpose would flow into our lives, filling all the spaces where sadness and pain now exist. Every day would be greeted with joy and anticipation at being useful.

Leo C. Rosten once said: "I cannot believe that the purpose of life is to be 'happy.' I think the purpose of life is to be useful, to be responsible, to be honorable, to be compassionate. It is, above all, to matter; to count, to stand for something, to have made some difference that you lived at all."[1]

When we offer ourselves to God and "go where He wants us to go,"[2] we find that God makes more of us than we ever dreamed possible. All we need is the willingness to serve.

1. Leo C. Rosten, address given at National Book Awards, March 1962, New York City; see *Library Journal*, 4 June 1962, 2075.
2. Mary Brown, "I'll Go Where You Want Me to Go," *Hymns of The Church of Jesus Christ of Latter-day Saints* (Salt Lake City: The Church of Jesus Christ of Latter-day Saints, 1985), no. 270.

Impulsive Behavior

WE OFTEN CHARACTERIZE IMPULSIVE BEHAVIOR as a negative thing. We equate it with acting rashly, hastily, or in an ill-advised fashion. To act impulsively is to buy something we don't need on a whim—and pay too much for it. It is to change drastically our appearance during a moment of depression. It is to raise our voice in passing anger at someone who doesn't deserve it. It is to break down at the last minute and eat that éclair we've been resisting all day long. It is to make an important decision quickly, without gathering information beforehand. And, since we are human, impulsive behavior is something most of us will probably engage in at one time or another.

There is, however, an upside to our very mortal tendency to do something on the spur of the moment. There are those impulses that *should* be acted upon—freely, joyfully, and completely without guilt.

One woman was well known among her friends and associates for sending flowers. Instead of coming on predictable dates, such as birthdays and anniversaries, however, the tumble of flowers always arrived unexpectedly with a simple handwritten note that said, "Just thinking of you." When asked what prompted this lovely act, the woman said: "If somebody's on your mind, that's a sign you should do something—call, visit, drop a line. Maybe what you do won't make a difference to that person—but maybe it will."

One ninety-three-year-old gentleman remembers well an "impulsive" gesture that made all the difference. He was driving out of town on a cold Wyoming night during the years of the Great Depression, when he saw the man who worked as a cook for one of the local ranchers walking alongside the road. On pure impulse, he pulled over and asked if the cook needed a lift. The cook readily accepted.

As the two men drove along the lonely stretch of landscape, a sorry story emerged. The cook, who was of a different race and religion, had been threatened by the ranch hands. Fearing for his life, he left with only the clothes on his back. Moved by his tale, the driver went to another town fifty miles south, cleaned out his wallet, and gave the contents to the cook with every wish for success, thinking he would never see him again.

As it turned out, the cook found himself another job in a restaurant, where he established himself as a solid worker, and whenever the man who'd rescued him from that cold Wyoming night passed through town, he always had a warm meal on the house.

May we all continue to act on those impulses that bless our lives and the lives of the people around us!

The Simple Acts of Love

THERE IS A THOUGHT-PROVOKING SAYING that poses the question, "What have you done in the world for heaven's sake?" To some, the thought may suggest active and visible involvement in some grandiose cause that will gain the world's attention. It is likely, however, that heaven does not need a world of noisy activists as much as it needs a world of souls who love through quiet, simple acts. That is where the real difference happens, and it happens so gently that we often are not aware of its significance—particularly when we are the ones performing the acts.

Such was the case with one woman whose elderly mother was ill and needing her help at the same time her mentally impaired daughter was involved in a program that required the woman's participation as well. One day, after helping her aged mother and then stopping off to assist her daughter, she came home weary and exhausted. That evening she became aware of a service project her community was sponsoring and wished to participate but had no strength nor time left. She told her husband she felt bad that she was so busy she didn't even have time to do some good in the world. He smiled at the irony and said, "My dear, every act of love you do for your mother and our daughter is the greatest good you could possibly do in the world."

Spencer W. Kimball said, "So often our acts of service consist of simple encouragement or of giving mundane help with mundane tasks . . . but what glorious consequences can flow from mundane acts and from small but deliberate deeds!"[1]

Another such deed was recently observed in an airport terminal. A man and woman, waiting for their flight which had been delayed several hours, noticed a young mother scheduled for the same flight struggling with her twin toddlers. They saw her frustration and began to play with the children—first with a peek-a-boo game, then with paper and pen—and finally the time to board arrived. They assisted the mother and children onto the plane, where the woman then exchanged seats with another passenger so that she could be more available to help with the children during the flight. The young mother was deeply touched by their caring and said, "Thank you so much. I really needed you."

If we could tune in to heaven during such times, we might also hear a Divine Being gratefully saying, "Thank you so much. I really needed you." The quiet, mundane service we give to others, including our own families, is of great value. One future day we may be quite surprised to discover how significant and heaven-like this service really is.

---

1. Spencer W. Kimball, *The Teachings of Spencer W. Kimball* (Salt Lake City: Bookcraft, 1982), 252.

"Greater Love Hath No Man Than This"

ALMOST 2,000 YEARS AGO Jesus Christ taught His disciples: "Greater love hath no man than this, that a man lay down his life for his friends."[1] Yet, history seems to suggest that relatively few mortals ever express this ultimate form of love. Courageous servicemen have died in battle because of their love for country. Devoted mothers have offered their lives to protect one of their children. And political and religious leaders have been martyred for their beliefs. But what of each of us in the common circumstances of our daily routines?

Perhaps our sacrifices of smaller scale actually add up to expressions of greater love. For in a very real sense, we lay our lives down every time we put the interests and needs of another ahead of our current cares and pressing responsibilities. Though we may not suffer a martyr's fate, be killed in combat, or exchange our life for a family member's safety, certain daily occurrences offer countless opportunities to lay down our lives, not in death but in service—one day, one hour, one moment at a time.

A hurried housewife leaves her shopping cart on the side of a supermarket aisle and takes ten minutes to reunite a lost child with a worried mother. A busy student puts his studies aside for an hour to listen to a friend's troubles. A family donates one day of its summer vacation to serve meals and distribute blankets at a local homeless shelter. An elderly widow's fingers forget their arthritis long enough to pen a simple note of thanks.

Each day offers us opportunities to lay down our lives in small ways, to perform minor miracles, and to change lives as we cultivate this greater love. Often it is the smallest, simplest acts that brighten a day, lift a burden, or heal a hidden wound—a kind word to a fellow worker, a courtesy extended to a stranger, an hour of attention carved out of a strenuous schedule.

When we lay our lives down to help others, even anonymously, our ability to love increases. And, miraculously, when we return to our own problems, they seem lighter and easier to bear after shouldering the burdens of others.

Whether we give our lives in one decisive instant or a few moments at a time over a handful of decades, the results are the same. We learn that sacrifice can overshadow self, for one cannot lovingly serve others without being personally lifted by the very act. Whether in life or in death, the road to true happiness is paved with service. And somewhere along the journey, we realize that we have developed the capacity both to give and to receive greater love.

1. *New Testament,* John 15:13.

· SIMPLICITY ·

Life Is in the Details

A POPULAR PHRASE TODAY IS "Don't sweat the small stuff." But, in fact, life *is* made up of small stuff—little details that combine, like stitches in a tapestry, to make a work of art.

Think of the little things that have meant so much to you—the encouragement you still remember from a teacher or coach; the compliment that made you believe in your abilities; the flowers or phone call that arrived just as you were feeling your lowest; the bedtime stories whispered in your ear; the uncle who took you to the carnival; the baby-sitter who let you make green eggs and ham; the neighbor who never forgets your birthday.

To the giver, these little moments seem almost insignificant. But, to the receiver, the ever so small can be infinitely important when done just at the right moment. Small events can make the difference in whom we marry, what career we choose, and what we do with our lives.

Christ spoke of faith—the size of a grain of mustard seed—being able to move mountains.[1] He also said, "Out of small things proceedeth that which is great."[2] Little things don't take much effort, yet the dividends are enormous: a loving note tucked into a child's lunchbox; a cup of hot chocolate brought to a teen-ager who's staying up late to study; trash cans brought in for a neighbor; a few minutes rubbing the shoulders of a weary spouse. Every small act of kindness indelibly etches us into the heart of another.

Even being able to admit our mistakes teaches our children that they, too, can admit when they are wrong. A boy can learn to forgive when he sees his father forgive someone who cheated him in his business. A girl who sees her mother take a meal to a poor family down the road learns an indelible lesson in generosity.

Don't hold back because you think your gift is meaningless. Remember the details of your own life's tapestry—some of the smallest events were some of your most important moments. If one candle can light a thousand others, one act of kindness can, indeed, make a world of difference to someone else.

1. *New Testament,* Matthew 17:20.
2. *Doctrine and Covenants* 64:33.

Simple Things in a Disposable World

WE LIVE IN AN AGE OF INNOVATION, where almost daily new discoveries lengthen our lives, enlarge our vocabularies, and change the way we travel, work, and communicate. In our rapidly changing world, state-of-the-art computers, improved medicines, and new cars constantly roll off the assembly line—only to quickly become obsolete. With so much change and complexity surrounding us, is it any wonder that we occasionally need to be reminded of the simple and unchanging things that make life worth living?

While technology races on, some of the most profound discoveries are still the most simple—and usually they await us within the walls of our own homes. For example, in today's world we are flooded with information and surrounded by entertainment options; hundreds of television channels and dozens of publications compete for our time and attention. Yet, wisely, many families have learned to turn off the TV in order to spend more time together, rediscovering the art of conversation and the importance of togetherness. Taking the time to talk with your spouse, to read a bedtime story with a three-year-old son, or listen to a teenage daughter's concerns are simple things, really, but they are opportunities that cable TV and the remote control cannot afford us.

Similarly, medical science still cannot explain why newborn infants need to be held or how individuals beyond a physician's help come out of a coma in response to the voices of loved ones. But perhaps, as a French scientist reflected: "Someday, after we have mastered the winds, the waves, the tides, and gravity, we will harness for God the energies of love; and then, for the second time in the history of the world, man will have discovered fire."[1]

In today's world of cellular phones, satellite dishes, and e-mail addresses, isn't it remarkable that the purpose and simplicity of prayer remain unchanged, inviting, and indispensable. When we pray, we never get an answering machine or a busy signal. Our Heavenly Father loves us and He listens to us. Our humble supplications and expressions of gratitude are heard in the heavens— always without directory assistance or long-distance charges.

And although our mail boxes and phone lines fill with advertisements for new products, we tend to treasure the unexpected call from a caring relative or the handwritten note from an old friend. They are simple things, really; but they teach us that, while yesterday's inventions may be disposable, our loved ones and families are not. Today's fashions will change, and soon the best computer chips and cellular phones will be obsolete; but even in a disposable world, the simple things of life—like love and friendship, gratitude and prayer—will never become outdated.

---

1. Teilhard de Chardin, in Barbara B. Smith, "Love Is Life," *The New Era*, February 1986, 50.

The Glory of an Ordinary Day

SOMETIMES IT TAKES A SERIOUS JOLT in life to open our eyes and see the glory of an ordinary day. Such was the case of one woman who recently faced a life-threatening illness. Through major surgery, though disfiguring, her life has been prolonged. Those who call to give her comfort are surprised when they hear her say that she is so blessed that each morning when she awakes she is so happy and thankful to be alive. For this woman, every ordinary day is now an extraordinary day that she greets with hope and enthusiasm.

Writer Mary Jean Irion helps us see the deeper perspective: "Normal day, let me be aware of the treasure you are. Let me learn from you, love you, savour you, bless you before you depart. Let me not pass you by in quest of some rare and perfect tomorrow. Let me hold you while I may."[1] So we may ask, "How do we *love, savour,* and *bless* a normal day?"

The answers surround us and, because of their simplicity, they often escape us. To "savour" a normal day, we can begin with the simple act of opening the shades that give privacy in the night and let in the morning rays of light. To sit, even for a moment, in that light and thank our Divine Creator for another new day can sharpen our ability to find joy. We are then ready to learn from, to love, and to bless that normal day, however ordinary it may be.

It can be done as simply as responding to the child who says, "Please read me a story" and then savoring the sight of the child's happy face as we read. It can happen by saying "I love you" to someone we love or smiling and chatting with the stranger in line at the store. It can also happen by thanking an employee for a job well done and, in each case, enjoying the happy response.

It can happen as we feel lifted by the strains of a favorite song or as we notice the budding of a new flower, the freshness in the air after a rain, or the reflection of light on the clouds as the evening sun bids farewell. It can happen by recounting just a few of the good things that filled our day as we kneel in evening prayer and thank a loving Father, who gave us one more ordinary day.

1. Mary Jean Irion, in *The Harper Book of Quotations* (New York City: Harper Perennial, 1993), 266.

The Business of Children

HAVE YOU EVER WATCHED a young child at play? But is it really play? What we call play can be serious business to a child. Watch a child listening to the dial tone on a telephone or touching the prickly ends of a fir tree or catching snowflakes in gloved hands. These are simple things that we, as adults, take for granted. But to the child, the sound, the feel, the sight is pure delight.

We can dismiss the whole thing, saying that to the child these things are new—while we've heard the dial tone more times than we've wanted to, we've encountered pricklier things like cacti, and snowflakes melt so fast. Why bother? But is it really the newness that captures a child's delight? Or does the delight come because the child is paying attention?

Unfortunately, we may see something so often that we no longer see it at all. Yet, our connections with the people and things around us come by paying attention—close attention.

One woman arrived home from a stressful day at work, complete with bumper-to-bumper traffic on the way home. She was feeling alone and tired. As she walked through the door—the same door she had walked through every day for years—she suddenly noticed how the setting sun coming through the window shone on the painting of an Easter lily that hung in the living room. She stopped, noticing the yellow inside of the flower against the rubbery white and seeing how the light brightened the green of the stem and made the white purer. In that moment she felt somehow connected to both the talent God had given the artist and to the beauty God had placed in the world. It was only a moment of paying attention, but to her surprise, she could feel herself beginning to heal from the day's wounds.

Now that isn't a miracle reserved for a chosen few. Paying careful attention to things and people around us can help heal anyone who is willing to assume the serious business of children. By learning to pay childlike attention to life, pain can become experience, touch can become lasting sensation, suffering can become a future guide, and the simplest moments can become great delights.

Days Lived Well

SOME PEOPLE JUST SEEM to have a passion for living—an enthusiasm for life that makes each day full of zest and meaning. Their happiness isn't a function of age, education, income, or experience. And when you examine their lives more closely, you'll find they're ordinary people who through willpower, determination, and faith find joy amid life's daily challenges. These "everyday" enthusiasts have an amazing ability to both recognize and dwell on the positive.

One such positive thinker battled an inferiority complex during his life. As a college student, he recalled that his shyness made him tongue-tied and embarrassed when called to speak in public. But with practice and faith, Norman Vincent Peale went on to become one of the nation's most loved ministers and writers. Delivering hundreds of sermons and writing a score of books, he has inspired countless others to believe in God and in themselves. To the end of his 95 years, he was passionate about his message of hope. He wrote: "Every month is a new beginning. So is every day. Perhaps that is why God brings down the curtain of night—to blot out the day that is done. All of your yesterdays ended last night. It makes no difference how long you've been alive, they're all ended. This day is absolutely new. You've never lived it before. What an opportunity!"[1]

Some scoff at the simplicity of the message. But truth, though not necessarily easy, is frequently simple. Yes, life is difficult at times. But in spite of the heartache and sorrow, there can be joy and hope. Each day is given to us as a precious gift. We can feel enthusiasm for the glories in it: laugh with a giggling child, bask in a ray of sunshine, hum a favorite tune, hold the hand of a loved one. And day by day, our lives will be more full.

On the wall of Norman Vincent Peale's study at the church where he was minister for over fifty years hung his lifelong motto: "Trust God and live a day at a time." After all, life is just a collection of days. And one simple thing done well today, or kindly expressed, or sincerely enjoyed can make the difference in this day—and add meaning and enthusiasm to life.

1. Norman Vincent Peale, *Have a Great Day—Every Day* (Old Tappan, New Jersey: Foundation for Christian Living and Fleming H. Revell Company, 1985), 38.

· S P I R I T U A L I T Y ·

The Still Small Voice

AND THE LORD SAID: "Go forth, and stand upon the mount of the Lord. And behold, the Lord passed by, and a great and strong wind rent the mountains, and brake in pieces the rocks before the Lord; but the Lord was not in the wind: and after the wind an earthquake; but the Lord was not in the earthquake: And after the earthquake a fire; but the Lord was not in the fire; and after the fire a still small voice."[1]

How marvelous that a loving Father in Heaven, with all His power, majesty, and might, chooses to speak to His children in a still small voice of gentle persuasion. Still small voices respect our right to make choices. Still small voices require a listening ear.

In addition to winds, earthquakes, and fires, there are other things that keep us from hearing the still small voice of the Lord. We live in a time when many influences compete for our time and attention. We are bombarded by information coming at us at staggering rates. We can hardly keep up with it all. At the end of some days, we may feel like we've been in a terrible accident on the information superhighway.

And yet, information—no matter how fast it comes to us— does not in itself bring wisdom. If we are not careful, we may find ourselves ever learning, but never able to come to the knowledge of the truth.[2]

Many of us move from one impossible deadline to another. And yet, for all our running, once in a while we need to call *time out*. Time spent in quiet contemplation is never wasted. As the poet Shelley expressed, "I love tranquil solitude and such society as is quiet, wise and good."[3]

What can we do to prepare ourselves for hearing the still small voice of the Lord? Simple things, really. Taking a walk in the park. Setting aside time to pray. Visiting a friend who's been ill. Reading the scriptures. Tending a garden. Making a gift for a neighbor. Writing a letter of appreciation. Listening to a bird. Going to church. Listening to the laughter of a small child. Making a list of our blessings.

Taking time to listen for the Lord's voice is not just another chore to be added to an already busy schedule. Like adding leaven to bread, we will find that it gives vitality to everything else we do.

We would all do well to listen for the still small voice of the Lord.

1. *Old Testament,* 1 Kings 19:11–12.
2. *New Testament,* 2 Timothy 3:7.
3. Percy Bysshe Shelley, "Rarely, Rarely, Comest Thou, Spirit of Delight," in *19th-Century Literature Criticism,* 18:340, 344, 371.

Pondering

IN OUR LIVES, FULL OF NOISE and turmoil and conflict, opportunities for quiet pondering may seem limited. Among the jangling rings of a telephone, the insistent questions of a child, the pressures of schedules, the rush of the day, there may not seem to be time for thought gathering and peaceful reflection. But when our time seems most crowded and cluttered, we need to take a moment to think, to reflect, to ponder.

Christ requested of His disciples that they not just listen to His words, but as He put it, "go unto your homes, and ponder upon the things which I have said,"[1] Truly, to attempt to understand the thoughts and intents of God requires more than a simple reading of scripture or a hastily offered prayer. Likewise, important matters that we deal with day to day require a time of quiet reflection and thought, pondering deeply both our most intensely felt questions and the answers we are led to.

As we ponder, we cleanse our mind of the clutter that accumulates during the day. We set in order our thoughts and make the connections that perhaps lead us to look at things in a new light.

Pondering may also include reading. Time spent with the scriptures, doors closed and phone disconnected, can help place the mundane routine of life into sharper perspective and give us much-needed comfort. A few moments alone with our thoughts—to ponder, to reflect—can perhaps help to solve insurmountable problems, to rethink a hasty decision, or to cope with daily challenges.

If we would but take the time, the most trying events in our lives can come into focus and, in turn, we, too, can find peace. When we feel most overwhelmed by life, let us follow the scriptures to "[keep] all these things, and ponder them in [our] heart."[2]

---

1. *The Book of Mormon,* 3 Nephi 17:3.
2. *New Testament,* Luke 2:19.

Spirituality

Seek for the Light

Most of us, from the moment we awake, seek for sources of light. We intuitively switch on a lamp to brighten a room, or we make our way to a window and crack open the blinds. We may even leave the comfortable confines of our home altogether to enjoy the light of a new day.

When warmed by the sun's radiant rays, we sometimes ponder the marvel of this seemingly endless source of light, and we may even pause to remember one of the earliest of all the acts of creation, when God declared, "Let there be light . . . and [He] saw the light, that it was good."[1]

Our thoughts may then turn to other connections between the light and the good as we consider that those forces which are pure, uplifting, and inspiring are commonly associated with light; while those that drag us down, that distract us from our chosen course, that denigrate those things we hold sacred are often symbolized by darkness.

We may even recall times when our own journeys have been obscured by unwelcome clouds and gloom that have caused us to hope for the day when the way would become more clear.

Whether we find ourselves caught in overwhelming darkness or simply needing to brighten a day, the scriptures give us this promise: "That which is of God is light,"[2] "the true light, which lighteth every man that cometh into the world."[3]

And with that as our promise, we are also given the charge to "Walk while ye have the light, lest darkness come upon you."[4]

We each have the opportunity to decide daily how best to find and then care for the light that has been given to us. And, whenever we find ourselves looking to add to our light, we have the unending assurance of a loving God, who has promised to stand always as "a lighthouse that throws its beam upon the ocean of the eternal."[5]

151

1. *Old Testament,* Genesis 1:3–4

2. *Doctrine and Covenants* 50:24.

3. *New Testament,* John 1:9.

4. *New Testament,* John 12:35.

5. Albert Schweitzer, *The Spiritual Life: Selected Writings of Albert Schweitzer,* ed. Charles R. Joy (Hopewell, New Jersey: The Ecco Press, 1996), 230.

Day of Rest

O N THE SEVENTH DAY," the Bible tells us, "God . . . rested . . . from all his work which he had made." The idea of a Sabbath, of a day in which mankind rests from his labors, is an idea that goes back to the beginning of time itself. "And God blessed the seventh day, and sanctified it."[1]

The historian Paul Johnson has said that "the day of rest is one of the . . . great contributions to the comfort and joy of mankind."[2] Indeed, it is hard to imagine how we could possibly cope without it. As life seems to move faster and faster each day— every hour and every minute filled with obligations and responsibilities and worries—our need for a day of rest, of meditation and peace, is perhaps greater than ever before in history.

To many of our ancestors, the Sabbath was a day of joyless prohibitions, of tedious "thou shalts," and of restrictive "thou shalt nots." But to the great rabbis of ancient Israel, the Sabbath was intended as a time of joy. We read in the Talmud that men should "delight in the Sabbath," suggesting that, to those who did, "shall God give inheritance without end."[3]

The writer Ian Frazier, shortly after the death of his parents, decided to research and write a book about his family history as far back as he could trace it. As he neared the end of his task, it occurred to him that the most important lesson he had learned from it was the importance of keeping the Sabbath. "Not," wrote

Frazier, "in the sense that you must never mail a letter on Sunday, but in the sense that every person should spend a certain amount of time thinking about what he or she believes."[4]

Of course, the Sabbath is a day of rest. But we should remember that it is a day ordained by God to rest through worship, prayer, and service. Above all, it is a day to reaffirm, in the profoundest sense, who we are and what we believe. When we do so, we will find that we, too, have sanctified God's holy day. And we will experience that joy which is the most peaceful kind of rest.

1. *Old Testament*, Genesis 2:2–3.
2. Paul Johnson, *A History of the Jews* (New York City: Harper and Row, 1987), 37.
3. *The Talmud: Selections*, translated by H. Polano (London and New York City: Frederick Warne and Company, 1876), 278.
4. Ian Frazier, *Family* (New York City: Farrar Strauss Giroux, 1994), 348.

"Wet Paint"

NO MATTER WHO WE ARE or where we come from, we all react to certain warning signs the same way. We all know to pull over when we hear a siren. None of us would ignore the shout of "Fire!" or a call for help. Likewise, we all know the symbol for poison.

It is tragic, however, that so few of us recognize spiritual warning signs. Yet, because they are easier to ignore, we often pay them no attention. It is as if we sometimes walk right past a "wet paint" sign, sit down on a freshly painted park bench, so to speak, and walk off with paint-striped clothing.

Great danger can be found in watching movies or reading material which extols immorality. It is a wet paint that colors our very souls, eating away at our essence like poison taken in small increments. Offensive words and actions soon become acceptable. Eventually they find their way into our personal behavior.

The desire for material wealth can also be a spiritual warning sign. While riches can be used to bless others, most of us are tempted to spend extra money on luxuries for ourselves. Soon we become proud of our designer labels, our expensive cars, our opulent homes. We feel disdainful of those who have less taste or sophistication. We forget Christ's warning not to oppress "the widow, nor the fatherless, the stranger, nor the poor."[1]

Self-pity is also a spiritual warning sign. It is a wet paint that covers our windows, making it impossible to see outside ourselves. When we feel sorry for ourselves, we become self-absorbed and negative. We fail to take action that could solve our problems and blame others for our misery. We become useless to the world, when one of life's purposes is to be useful.

If certain magazines, music, fashions, and attitudes came with bold warning signs, we might more easily avoid "the contagion of the world's slow stain,"[2] as the great English poet Shelley once described it. Instead, these dangers come disguised as pleasure, success, and entitlement.

We must see with spiritual eyes what is hidden from common view. When anything pulls us further away from our Father in Heaven, rather than inspires us to grow closer to Him, perhaps we can imagine a bold "Wet Paint" sign, warning us that even one brush against such hazard could leave us spotted and soiled. Let us step carefully and avoid all dangers—even those which bear no labels.

---

1. *Old Testament,* Zechariah 7:10.
2. Percy Bysshe Shelley, *Adonais* (New York City: Twayne Publishers, 1969), 140.

· TOLERANCE ·

Seeing Others through God's Eyes

Gᴏᴅ'ꜱ ɢʀᴇᴀᴛ ʟᴏᴠᴇ ꜰᴏʀ ᴜꜱ ꜱᴛᴇᴍꜱ not only from what we are today but also from what we can become tomorrow. In spite of our many imperfections, God offers each one of us hope, mercy, forgiveness, and the chance to change the things we don't like about our lives. Similarly, God expects us to look past the mistakes and weaknesses of others and to begin to love them not only for who they are but also for what they have the potential to become.

When we choose to see others as God sees them, we treat them with kindness and respect. And as we do, understanding replaces malice, forgiveness overcomes bitterness, and compassion dispels indifference. It has been said that we should be kind to the aged, patient with the young, forgiving of the weak and the wayward, and tolerant of the misguided and the foolish—for at some time in life, we will all be each of these things.

Kindness is not easy, asking for forgiveness and forgiving others can be a struggle, and unselfishness requires sacrifice; but, over time, we learn to value those virtues that make us go beyond ourselves and enable us to see things as they really are.

Nearly 2,000 years ago the Lord explained that our actions toward "the least of our brethren"[1] are the most telling barometer of what we think of Him. During His life, He manifest His

155

wondrous love for all who came into contact with Him. Each held His attention, received His help, and felt His love. In the crowds that surrounded Him, the Savior did not see beggars and invalids, sinners and sick people; instead, He saw those for whom He had come to give His life.

Our love of God is not measured by how humbly we will bow when we stand before Him, but rather by how we treat our fellowmen in His absence. It is what we do with our "daily slice of humanity"—the people whom life places in our path every day—that determines who we are and defines our relationships with God and man. Although it is difficult to be compassionate and caring in a world increasingly self-absorbed and insensitive, the scriptures promise that the pure in heart—who see the world not as it is but as it can be—will see God not only in heaven but also in all those who surround their daily walk on earth.

1. *New Testament,* Matthew 25:40.

The Universal Similarities of Mankind

WE LIVE IN A WORLD OF GREAT DIVERSITY, and yet there is a universal sameness that transcends international borders. Sometimes we get so caught up in our differences as nations that we forget to notice how much we, as human beings, are alike. Hearing the pure, sweet voices of a magnificent boys' choir from Latvia reminds us of these similarities. Each child represents a people who sacrifice for and love their children—just as we do. As wars break out in diverse parts of the globe, we become aware that each soldier who goes into battle has a family back home who loves him and prays for his safe return—just as we do when our loved ones are in danger.

One retired American couple, upon completing a mission of mercy to Nigeria, said: "We were strangers in a strange land, and yet we felt at home there. Those dear people loved us, and we could see how much they loved each other. And we loved them."

Another couple, after spending months in the frigid settlements of Siberia, reported that they were received with open arms by people who care about their families—a people willing to learn and improve their difficult circumstances.

A family, hosting a college student from mainland China, watched him as he studied to improve his own opportunities for the future and were inspired by his dedication and his concern for his family back home. Though he was raised in a completely different culture, it was obvious that his values were very much like their own.

Recently the compassionate life of a woman from Bolivia was brought to the attention of a large national organization of women. Her devotion in caring for others speaks loudly of the humanitarian nature of people everywhere.

The similarities of people of all nations exist because, in the words of John Donne, "All mankind is of one author, and is one volume."[1] We come from a common Father in Heaven, who is the core of what makes us so much alike in what really matters. His love is everywhere, and it is obvious that He has tenderly placed it into the hearts of all of His children. It is up to each of us to nurture that love and enjoy the similarities we share, wherever in the world we may be.

1. John Donne, "Meditation No. 17, Devotions upon Emergent Occasions," *Complete Poetry and Selected Prose of John Donne* (New York City: Random House, 1952), 440.

A Coat of Many Colors

AT FIRST GLANCE, PEOPLE VARY greatly from one another. We speak different languages, we claim various religions, we belong to differing cultures, and we come in countless colors. Even someone who may have grown up next door to us has different tastes, habits, and opinions. Ask newly married couples, who have made the "startling" discovery that their mates are not exactly like them! Truly, we are all individuals—all unique.

These differences may lead to conflict—from marital discord to international wars—if we allow them to divide us rather than letting similarities unite us.

If we feel threatened by the differences we find in others, we fall victim to prejudice. We judge unfairly. Yet, how can we gather strength with others to combat evil if we avoid everyone who is different than we are? Christ admonished His followers to be as one—united, not divided.[1]

Humorist Will Rogers once traveled the world and came back with the conclusion that, wherever they are, people are pretty much the same.[2] Another man, who devotes each Sunday to teaching inmates in prison, reached the same conclusion. Both men learned to look beyond color and custom and found that, inside, we are much more alike than different.

All human beings need love and acceptance. All of us need shelter, food, and safety. We each were blessed with talents; yet, we all make mistakes. We all experience both joy and sorrow, the need to forgive and be forgiven, and the dreams and hopes for a better future.

When conflicts come, whether in a personal relationship or in a broader social struggle, remember the areas of common ground—how much alike we are, instead of how different. Are we not all brothers and sisters, children of a loving Heavenly Father? Keeping this in mind is often the key to a happy marriage, a synchronized community, and even compatible terms between opposing governments.

This is what harmony is—people singing different parts, but learning to blend together. Without differences, there would be no harmony. Just imagine a painting of only one color or a menu of only one food. If everyone in our lives were an exact replica of us, there would be no growth, no challenge, no new ideas to delight our senses. We would be living in a house of mirrors.

Differences, in fact, should be celebrated, not resented. William Wrigley, Jr. said, "When two men in a business always agree, one of them is unnecessary."[3] Life is richer when we rejoice in the variety that God has created, rather than try to bend all others to fit into one shoe size.

Let us not fear differences, but welcome them. After all, to someone else, we are the unusual one. Let us show tolerance, even excitement, when we discover differences, for they form a beautiful mosaic which honors the intricate world our Father in Heaven has created—His own coat of many colors.

---

1. *New Testament,* John 17:20–26, Acts 4:32, Romans 12:5, Corinthians 1:10, and Ephesians 4:4–6.
2. Will Rogers, *The Value of Humor: The Story of Will Rogers* (La Jolla, California: Value Communications, Inc., 1976), 35.
3. William Wrigley Jr., in *The Forbes Scrapbook of Thoughts* (New York City: Forbes, Inc., 1968), 196.

Finding Common Ground

EACH OF US IS UNIQUE—a bit different from every other person in the world. That originality, that one-of-a-kindness, is a deliberate part of our creation. How marvelous to think that God made each of us in His own image, yet gave everyone distinct, individual traits.

Occasionally, we lose sight of this common ground—that we are all children of a loving Father in Heaven—and we let our differences lead to disagreements. Ironically, in nearly every conflict both parties have forgotten that they are much more alike than they are different.

Even among believers of different faiths there is sometimes unnecessary friction, when we could be celebrating what we both accept instead of seeking conflict over what we do not. If people could focus upon their shared beliefs, encouraging and applauding one another, think of the power we could generate. When we join forces for the benefit of all, we build strength—the kind of strength that accomplishes great things in the world.

If we remember that we do not need to be exactly alike to be united, we can blend our efforts to make a mighty difference. Patricia Holland said, "There are many things over which we can be divided, but one thing is needful for our unity—the empathy and compassion of the living Son of God."[1]

Throughout history, societies have learned that tolerance is essential if people are to live in peace. As long ago as 477 B.C., delegates from dozens of Greek city-states put aside their differences to form the Delian League, an alliance which joined forces to guard against Persian invasions. The result of their cooperation has become known as the Golden Age of Athens.[2]

While these days are past, we can create a Golden Age of our own if, when we meet others who are different than we—whether they are of another faith, another race, or another culture—we look with joy for the similarities. Let us find the points of agreement, the shared priorities, and join together in strength for those causes that unite us.

In Luke we read that, when we are not gathering, we are scattering.[3] Indeed, if we are not part of the harmony, we are part of the discord; our voice does not strengthen, but weakens the whole.

To make a real difference in the world around us, we need more than good individuals; we need good individuals linked with other good individuals. We must do more than tolerate the differences we find in others. We must view differences with gladness, knowing they are part of God's plan. Without them, we could not be the one-of-a-kind individuals we are: unique, yet with a wondrous common ground.

1. Patricia Holland, "One Thing Needful," *Ensign,* October 1987, 29.
2. *World History Patterns of Civilization* (Englewood Cliffs, New Jersey: Prentice Hall, 1993), 86.
3. *New Testament,* Luke 11:23.

A World with Only Robins

IMAGINE A WORLD IN WHICH the only birds are robins—no meadowlarks to serenade our morning walks, no ducks to delight us by their frolicking in the water, no blackbirds to scold us for walking in our own backyards, no penguins to amuse us by their bad imitation of waiters in fancy restaurants, and no eagles to inspire us as they soar above us on remote mountain trails.

There is nothing wrong with robins. But a world with only robins would, in comparison, be a dreary place.

In North America alone, there are eight hundred species of birds.[1] It is this variety that gives richness to life.

The same is true of us. We come in a variety of skin tones, customs, ethnic origins, languages, customs, and food preferences.

Just as a robin is no better than a bluebird, none of us is any better than anyone else. Does a robin speak badly of blue jays, make fun of orioles, or attempt to deny blue sky, ocean breezes, and rain to sparrows?

Let us learn to celebrate diversity. Let us take satisfaction in our heritage and the heritage of those around us.

The world is a more wonderful place because of ethnic diversity. For example, take a plate of Italian spaghetti. Pasta was developed in China and, according to legend, introduced to Europe by Marco Polo.[2] Tomatoes were first used by indigenous people in South America and taken to Europe from Mexico by explorers during the first half of the 16th century.[3]

Take away the pasta, leave out the tomatoes, or lose the recipe, and we are the worse off. If this is true for a simple plate of spaghetti, it is valid for more important aspects of life.

The simple fact is we need each other. Prejudice, racism, and disrespect for those different from us should have no place in our hearts. Whatever our differences, we have strong similarities—we love our children and we hope for their future. The common threads running through our lives should bring us closer together.

In many ways, we are like birds sharing a large shade tree— each greeting the sun with a slightly different, but still glorious, song. Let us seek to celebrate diversity and take satisfaction in our own heritage and that of our neighbors.

Let us learn to sing together.

1. *Field Guide to the Birds of North America* (Washington, D.C.: National Geographic Society, 1992), 6.
2. "Pasta," *Encyclopedia Americana,* deluxe library edition, 514.
3. "Tomato," *Encyclopedia Britannica, Micropedia,* 15th edition, 834.

Index

Index

Index

Index